easy food

photography by Jean Cazals

quadrille

First published in 2004 by
Quadrille Publishing Limited
Alhambra House
27-31 Charing Cross Road
London WC2H OLS

Reprinted in 2005 (twice)
10 9 8 7 6 5 4 3

Text and photographs © 1999 Quadrille Publishing Limited
and BBC Worldwide
Design and layout © 2004 Quadrille Publishing Limited

Some of the material in this volume was previously published in New Flavours

ISBN 1 84400 133 4

Creative Director Helen Lewis
Editorial Director Jane O'Shea
Consultant Editor Janet Illsley
Photographic Direction Vanessa Courtier
Senior Designer Jim Smith
Designer Ros Holder
Editor Jane Keskeys
Production Beverley Richardson

Printed in China

Cookery notes
All recipes serve 4 unless otherwise stated. All spoon measures are level
unless otherwise indicated. Follow either metric or imperial measures, not a
mixture of both as they are not necessarily interchangeable. Use fresh herbs
and freshly ground black pepper unless otherwise suggested.

Contents

easy
soups and
snacks

Mediterranean fish soup

Serves 4-6

900g/2lb mixed fish, such as
   monkfish, red mullet and
   mackerel, cleaned
225g/8oz raw tiger prawns
6 tbsp extra virgin olive oil
2 red onions, roughly chopped
2 garlic cloves, crushed
2 carrots, diced
1 celery stick, diced
4 tbsp brandy
1.2 litres/2 pints water

400g can chopped tomatoes
4 fresh rosemary sprigs
2 fresh bay leaves
¼ tsp saffron strands
salt and pepper

For the Parmesan crisps
100g/4oz Parmesan cheese, freshly
   grated

To finish
4-6 tbsp crème fraîche (optional)
paprika, for sprinkling

1 Preheat oven to 200C/fan oven 180C/Gas 6. Wash and dry the fish and cut into chunks, discarding the heads. Devein the prawns, and rinse well.
2 Heat 3 tbsp of the oil in a frying pan and fry the fish chunks and prawns in batches over a high heat until golden. Using a slotted spoon, transfer to a large saucepan.
3 Heat remaining oil in frying pan and gently fry the onions, garlic, carrots and celery for 10 minutes. Add the brandy and let bubble until evaporated.
4 Add the sautéed vegetables to the fish with the water, tomatoes, herbs and saffron. Slowly bring to the boil, skim, then cover and simmer for 30 minutes.
5 Meanwhile, make the Parmesan crisps. Sprinkle 4 small circles of grated cheese on a well oiled non-stick baking sheet. Bake for 3-4 minutes until crisp and golden. Leave on the baking sheet for 5 minutes, then carefully peel off using a palette knife. Repeat to make 16 crisps in total.
6 Purée the soup, including the seafood, in a blender or food processor until smooth. Pass through a fine sieve into a clean pan. Season and heat through.
7 Ladle the soup into warmed bowls. Drizzle with crème fraîche if wished, and sprinkle with paprika. Serve with the Parmesan crisps.

Parmesan crisps give this classic a new twist.

Chilled tomato soup with Thai flavours

Serves 6

700g/1½lb ripe tomatoes
2 garlic cloves, crushed
1 tsp grated fresh root ginger
4 lime leaves, shredded
2-4 red chillies, seeded and diced
2 spring onions, trimmed and
  chopped
2 tbsp chopped fresh coriander
300ml/½ pint iced water

150ml/¼ pint tomato juice
2 tbsp light soy sauce
2 tbsp rice wine vinegar
1 tbsp sesame oil
salt and pepper
To serve
ice cubes
torn coriander leaves
sesame oil

1 Roughly chop the tomatoes and place in a blender with the garlic, ginger, lime leaves, chillies, spring onions and coriander. Purée until fairly smooth.
2 Transfer to a large bowl and whisk in the water, tomato juice, soy sauce, wine vinegar and sesame oil. Season with salt and pepper to taste. Cover and chill in the refrigerator for several hours.
3 Serve with ice cubes, garnished with coriander and a drizzle of sesame oil.

An adaptation of classic Spanish gazpacho, using Thai ingredients. Make it during the summer, when tomatoes are full of flavour.

Pea soup with minted gremolata

Illustrated on previous pages

25g/1oz butter
1 onion, diced
1 potato, peeled and diced
450g/1lb shelled fresh peas (see note)
700ml/1¼ pints vegetable or chicken
    stock
2 fresh mint sprigs
salt and pepper

For the gremolata
2 tbsp shredded fresh mint leaves
grated rind of 1-2 lemons
1 garlic clove, crushed
To serve
extra virgin olive oil

1 Melt the butter in a pan, add the onion and potato and fry gently for
10 minutes until softened and lightly golden. Add the peas, stock, mint
and seasoning. Bring to the boil, lower the heat, cover and simmer gently
for 20 minutes.
2 Meanwhile, mix the gremolata ingredients together in a bowl.
3 Transfer the soup to a blender and purée until very smooth. Return
to the pan and heat through. Adjust the seasoning to taste.
4 Spoon the soup into warm bowls and serve topped with the gremolata
and a drizzle of olive oil.

Note Use frozen peas when fresh ones are out of season.

Gremolata – an Italian mix of mint, lemon zest
and garlic – adds a real zing to this creamy,
fresh tasting soup.

Fennel broth with anchovy croûtes

Serves 6

2 tbsp olive oil

1 onion, sliced

4 garlic cloves, crushed

grated rind of ½ orange

1 tbsp chopped fresh thyme

2 fennel bulbs, thinly sliced

2 tbsp Pernod

400g can chopped tomatoes

900ml/1½ pints fish stock

For the croûtes

6 thin slices French bread

50g/2oz can anchovy fillets, drained
  and chopped

25g/1oz pine nuts

1 garlic clove, crushed

2 tsp lemon juice

pepper

To finish

4 tbsp crème fraîche

fennel fronds or dill, to garnish

1 Preheat oven to 200C/fan oven 180C/Gas 6. Heat the olive oil in a saucepan, add the onion, garlic, orange rind, thyme and fennel, and fry gently for 10 minutes until the onion is softened and lightly golden. Add the Pernod and allow to bubble until it is evaporated.

2 Add the chopped tomatoes and stock, bring to the boil, cover and simmer gently for 30 minutes.

3 Meanwhile make the croûtes. Put the slices of French bread on a baking sheet and bake for 10 minutes until crisp and golden. Set aside.

4 Put the anchovy fillets, pine nuts, garlic, lemon juice and pepper in a blender or food processor and purée until fairly smooth. Spread the anchovy paste on top of the croûtes.

5 Spoon the fennel soup into warmed bowls and top each serving with an anchovy croûte. Add a spoonful of crème fraîche and garnish with a sprinkling of chopped fennel fronds or dill.

A fragrant fennel and fish broth topped with savoury anchovy croûtes.

Roasted tomato soup with ricotta

Serves 6
8 tbsp olive oil
1 onion, finely chopped
900g/2lb ripe tomatoes, halved
12 garlic cloves, peeled
15g/½oz fresh mint leaves
1 tsp caster sugar
salt and pepper

600ml/1 pint vegetable stock
100g/4oz dried pastina (small soup pasta)
For the garnish
50g/2oz ricotta cheese, crumbled
mint leaves
olive oil, to drizzle

1 Preheat oven to 220C/fan oven 200C/Gas 7. Heat half the oil in a shallow flameproof casserole and fry the onion for 10 minutes. Add the tomatoes, garlic cloves, mint, sugar, salt and pepper. Bring to the boil.
2 Transfer to the oven and roast, uncovered, for 20 minutes. Let cool slightly, then purée the tomato mixture with the remaining oil in a blender or food processor; return to the pan.
3 Stir in the stock and bring to the boil. Add the pasta and simmer gently for 10 minutes until al dente. Adjust the seasoning to taste.
4 Spoon into warmed bowls and top with crumbled ricotta, mint leaves and a generous drizzling of olive oil. Serve with Italian bread.

Roasted tomatoes give this hearty Italian tomato soup a great depth of flavour.

Mixed vegetable sushi

Illustrated on previous pages

225g/8oz sushi rice
3 tbsp rice wine vinegar
2 tbsp caster sugar
salt and pepper
2 eggs, lightly beaten
a little sunflower oil
8 sheets nori seaweed
140g/5oz mixed vegetables,
    including carrot, cucumber,
    cooked baby corn and cooked
    beetroot, cut into strips

To serve
wasabi paste
pickled ginger
Japanese soy sauce

1 Cook the rice according to pack instructions.
2 Warm the wine vinegar, sugar and 1½ tsp salt together in a small pan until dissolved.
3 Transfer the rice to a bowl and stir in the vinegar. Cover with a tea towel; leave to cool.
4 In another bowl, beat the eggs with a little salt and pepper. Brush an omelette pan with a little oil. Heat gently, pour in the egg and cook for 2 minutes until set. Cool, then cut into strips the same size as the vegetables.
5 Lay a sheet of seaweed on a bamboo mat or board and trim off the top third. Spread about 50g/2oz rice along the front end, flatten slightly, then place a line of omelette and vegetable strips on top. Roll up tightly to form a log. Cut into 5 or 6 slices.
6 Repeat with the remaining rice and vegetable strips to make a selection of different sushi fillings.
7 Arrange the sushi in individual bowls and serve accompanied by the wasabi, pickled ginger and soy sauce.

It's surprisingly easy to make your own sushi, and the ingredients are available from larger supermarkets as well as oriental food stores.

Roasted tomatoes on chick pea cakes

Serves 6

115g/4oz gram (chick pea) flour
1 tsp salt
450ml/16fl oz cold water
3 tbsp olive oil, plus extra for frying
24 large cherry tomatoes

1 garlic clove, crushed
4 fresh thyme sprigs
pinch of sugar
salt and pepper
1 tbsp balsamic vinegar
extra virgin olive oil, to serve

1 Preheat oven to 230C/fan oven 210C/Gas 8. Sift the flour and salt into a bowl. Gradually whisk in the water with 1 tbsp olive oil until smooth.
2 Turn into a non-stick pan and slowly bring to the boil, stirring constantly until the mixture is thickened enough to leave the side of the pan. Spoon into an oiled 23cm (9in) shallow cake tin. Set aside to cool.
3 Put the tomatoes, garlic, thyme and sugar in a small roasting tin; season with salt and pepper. Drizzle with remaining oil and roast for 20 minutes until softened. Sprinkle with the balsamic vinegar.
4 Turn out the chick pea 'cake' and cut into 6 wedges. Heat a little oil in a large frying pan and fry the chick pea wedges for 1-2 minutes each side until golden. Serve the chick pea wedges topped with the tomatoes and their juices, and a generous drizzle of extra virgin olive oil.

Similar to set polenta but with a smoother texture, chick pea wedges are the ideal base for juicy, roasted tomatoes.

Piadina with red mullet and aïoli

Serves 6

For the piadina
225g/8oz plain flour
salt and pepper
15g/½oz butter
150ml/¼ pint warm water

For the aïoli
2 egg yolks
1 tbsp lemon juice

300ml/½ pint olive oil
2 garlic cloves, crushed

For the topping
2 tbsp extra virgin olive oil
6 small red mullet, filleted, or
  6 trout fillets
squeeze of lemon juice
few rocket leaves

1 Sift the flour and ½ tsp salt into a bowl, rub in the butter, then work in the water to form a soft dough. Knead for 10 minutes on a lightly floured surface until smooth. Wrap in cling film and rest for 30 minutes.

2 To make the aioli, put the egg yolks, lemon juice and seasoning in a food processor and pulse briefly. With the motor still running, slowly add the oil through the funnel until the aioli is glossy and thick. Turn into a bowl and stir in the crushed garlic.

3 Divide the dough into 6 pieces. Roll out each piece on a floured surface to a 18cm/7in round. Preheat a griddle or heavy frying pan and fry the breads, one at a time, for 1 minute. Turn and cook the underside for 30 seconds; keep warm.

4 Heat the oil in a frying pan and cook the fish fillets for 1-2 minutes each side. Season and flavour with a little lemon juice.

5 Top each piadina with 2 red mullet fillets (or 1 trout fillet), a spoonful of aioli and a few rocket leaves. Serve at once.

Piadina are Italian flat griddle breads, often served with a topping. Make them in advance and reheat in the oven to serve.

Smoked fish tartlets

Serves 8

450g/1lb ready-made shortcrust
  pastry
450g/1lb undyed smoked haddock
  fillet, skinned
200ml/7fl oz milk
2 strips of lemon zest
200ml/7fl oz double cream
2 medium eggs, lightly beaten
1 tbsp chopped fresh tarragon
pinch of cayenne pepper
salt and pepper
tarragon leaves, to garnish
salad leaves, to serve

1 Preheat oven to 200C/fan oven 180C/Gas 6. Divide the pastry into 8 pieces.
Roll out on a lightly floured surface into thin rounds and use to line eight
10cm/4in individual flan tins. Prick the bases with a fork and chill in the
refrigerator for 30 minutes.

2 Line the pastry cases with greaseproof paper and baking beans and bake
blind for 15 minutes; remove the paper and beans and bake for a further
10-15 minutes until the pastry is crisp and golden. Set aside to cool.

3 Place the fish in a shallow pan with the milk and lemon strips. Bring
to a gentle simmer, cover and poach gently for 7 minutes. Cool slightly,
then flake the fish discarding any bones. Leave to cool.

4 Put the fish in a bowl with the cream, eggs, tarragon, cayenne and salt
and pepper. Stir gently to mix.

5 Spoon the filling into the flan cases and bake for 25 minutes until risen
and set. Leave to cool slightly for a few minutes. Serve warm on a bed
of mixed salad leaves, garnished with tarragon sprigs.

Smoked fish works beautifully in these melt
in the mouth tartlets.

Smoked chicken and sweet onion wrap

1 tbsp olive oil
1 large red onion, sliced
1 red chilli, seeded and sliced
½ tsp salt
50g/2oz redcurrant jelly
1 tbsp red wine vinegar
4 large flour tortillas

2 handfuls of mizuna or other salad
leaves
225g/8oz smoked chicken (or cooked
breast fillet), shredded
1 small ripe avocado, peeled, stoned
and sliced
4 tbsp crème fraîche

1 Heat the oil in a frying pan, add the onion and chilli and fry over a medium heat for 10 minutes until browned. Add the salt, redcurrant jelly, vinegar and 1 tbsp water; cook gently for a further 15 minutes until thickened. Leave to cool.

2 Lay the tortillas flat and then top each one with a few salad leaves, the shredded chicken, avocado slices, a spoonful of the onion jam and a dollop of crème fraîche.

3 Carefully fold the tortilla around the filling to form a cone shape and wrap up firmly. Serve at once or wrap securely in napkins or waxed paper and keep in a cool place until ready to serve.

The sandwich of the moment, 'the wrap' is simply a tasty filling wrapped up in a Mexican soft flour tortilla.

Roasted chicken and spinach wrap

225g/8oz roasted chicken (off the
   bone)
4 large flour tortillas
50g/2oz young spinach leaves, stems
   removed

2 fresh peaches, halved, stoned and
   sliced
2 tbsp mayonnaise
2 tsp chopped fresh basil
freshly grated Parmesan, to taste

1 Cut the roast chicken into long, thin shreds.
2 Lay the tortillas flat on a clean surface and top each one with a handful
of spinach leaves. Scatter the shredded chicken and peach slices on top.
3 Mix the mayonnaise with the chopped basil and spoon on top of the
chicken. Grate over fresh Parmesan to taste.
4 Carefully fold the tortilla around the filling to form a cone shape and wrap
up firmly. Serve at once or wrap securely in waxed paper and keep in
a cool place until ready to serve.

Flour tortillas wrapped around a filling of
shredded chicken, tender spinach, peach slices
and chopped basil for a portable snack.

Pork and liver pâté with apple relish

100g/4oz chicken livers, diced
3 tbsp marsala
175g/6oz unsalted butter
3 shallots, finely chopped
2 garlic cloves, crushed
1 tbsp chopped fresh sage
¼ tsp cayenne pepper
100ml/3½fl oz pork or chicken stock
25g/1oz fresh breadcrumbs
225g/8oz cooked pork, diced
100g/4oz cooked ham, diced

salt and pepper
1 fresh sage sprig
For the apple relish
1 small onion, sliced
½ tsp grated fresh root ginger
1 large cooking apple, peeled, cored and diced
4 tbsp cider vinegar
4 tbsp water
5 tbsp light muscovado sugar

1 Put the chicken livers and marsala in a bowl, and leave to marinate for at least 15 minutes.

2 Melt 50g/2oz of the butter in a frying pan, add the shallots, garlic and sage and fry gently for 5 minutes. Add the chicken livers and marsala. Fry over a high heat for 1 minute, then stir in the cayenne and stock. Simmer for 3-4 minutes until the livers are cooked. Leave to cool completely.

3 Put the cooled mixture in a food processor with the breadcrumbs, pork and ham; work briefly to chop finely. Season to taste.

4 Spoon the mixture into a pâté dish and smooth the surface. Melt remaining butter over a low heat, let cool for 5 minutes, then carefully pour over the pâté. Position the sage sprig on top, pressing gently down into the butter. Chill for several hours.

5 Meanwhile, make the relish. Put all the ingredients in a pan and bring to the boil. Lower heat and simmer for 35-40 minutes until thickened. Cool and season to taste.

6 Serve the pâté with the relish and crisp French sticks.

A simple pâté set under a layer of butter, served with a tangy apple and ginger relish.

Bresaola antipasta

Illustrated on previous pages

50g/2oz good quality, large salted
  capers
1 tbsp plain flour
3 tbsp olive oil
3 tbsp fresh parsley leaves
squeeze of lemon juice
16 slices good quality bresaola
85g/3oz mixed mâche and rocket
  leaves
25g/1oz pecorino cheese shavings

For the dressing
½ small shallot, finely chopped
1 tsp white wine vinegar
½ tsp Dijon mustard
½ tsp sugar
4 tbsp extra virgin olive oil
salt and pepper

1 Soak the capers in cold water for 30 minutes. Drain and pat dry with kitchen paper, then dust with the flour.
2 Heat the oil in a small frying pan and fry the capers for 2-3 minutes until crisp and golden. Add the parsley leaves and fry for 30 seconds. Drain on kitchen paper, then toss the mixture with the lemon juice.
3 Whisk the dressing ingredients together in a bowl.
4 Arrange the bresaola on serving plates. Top with the salad leaves, caper mixture and pecorino shavings. Drizzle with the dressing and serve.

Cured beef, crisp capers and sweet/sharp pecorino cheese combine beautifully in this Italian starter.

Smoked duck antipasta

1 large smoked duck breast
75g/3oz mizuna or rocket leaves
50g/2oz bean sprouts
handful of coriander leaves
2 tsp toasted sesame seeds

For the dressing
2 tbsp sunflower oil
½ tsp sesame oil
1 tbsp lime juice
1½ tsp caster sugar
1 red chilli, seeded and chopped
salt

1 Thinly slice the duck breast and arrange on individual serving plates.
2 Top each serving with a handful of mizuna or rocket leaves, bean sprouts, a few coriander leaves and a sprinkling of toasted sesame seeds.
3 For the dressing, whisk together the sunflower oil, sesame oil, lime juice, caster sugar, red chilli and a pinch of salt.
4 Drizzle the dressing over the salads to serve.

Note If you are unable to buy whole smoked duck breast, look for a pack of sliced smoked duck breast in the supermarket chilled cabinet.

Fresh coriander, beansprouts, chilli and sesame flavours give this unusual antipasta an oriental twist.

Mini chicken kiev

Serves 2

2 large skinless chicken breast fillets

4 tbsp seasoned flour

1 large egg, lightly beaten

115g/4oz dried plain breadcrumbs

1 tbsp sesame seeds

sunflower oil, for shallow frying

For the spiced butter

50g/2oz butter, at room temperature

1 small red chilli, seeded and diced

½ tsp ground cumin

1 tbsp chopped fresh coriander

grated rind and juice of ½ lime

salt and pepper

To serve

lime wedges

1 Start by making the spiced butter. Place all the ingredients in a bowl and beat until well blended. Roll into a small log, wrap in foil and freeze for at least 1 hour.

2 Lay each chicken breast flat and slice in half horizontally to give 4 thin escalopes. Place between sheets of cling film and beat flat with a rolling pin.

3 Cut the chilled butter into 4 slices. Place 1 slice in the middle of each escalope and fold the chicken over the butter to enclose and seal. Secure with cocktail sticks.

4 Dust each parcel with flour, then dip into the egg. Mix the breadcrumbs and sesame seeds together. Carefully toss the chicken parcels in the crumb mixture and coat well. Chill for several hours, or overnight.

5 Heat a shallow layer of oil in a frying pan and gently fry the parcels for 15-20 minutes, turning several times, to brown evenly. Drain on kitchen paper and remove the cocktail sticks. Serve with lime wedges.

Serve these croquettes as a snack lunch or supper with a crisp salad.

Chicken liver and blueberry salad

4 tbsp extra virgin olive oil
50g/2oz whole unblanched almonds
sea salt and pepper
350g/12oz chicken livers, halved
  if large
175g/6oz blueberries

1 tbsp raspberry vinegar
100g/4oz mixed salad leaves
50g/2oz French beans, blanched
few fresh herb leaves (eg. basil,
  mint, parsley)

1 Heat 2 tbsp oil in a frying pan and fry the almonds gently until evenly browned. Remove with a slotted spoon, dust with sea salt and set aside.
2 Increase the heat. Add the chicken livers to the pan and fry for 1 minute. Turn and fry for a further 1 minute until browned on the outside, but still slightly pink in the middle. Remove and let rest for a few minutes.
3 Return the pan to the heat, add the blueberries and warm through for 30 seconds. Remove from the heat and add the remaining oil and the raspberry vinegar.
4 Arrange the salad leaves, beans, herbs and almonds on serving plates. Add the chicken livers, then spoon over the blueberries and pan juices. Serve at once, with warm bread.

Blueberries and a warm, fruity dressing perfectly offset rich chicken livers.

easy
pasta

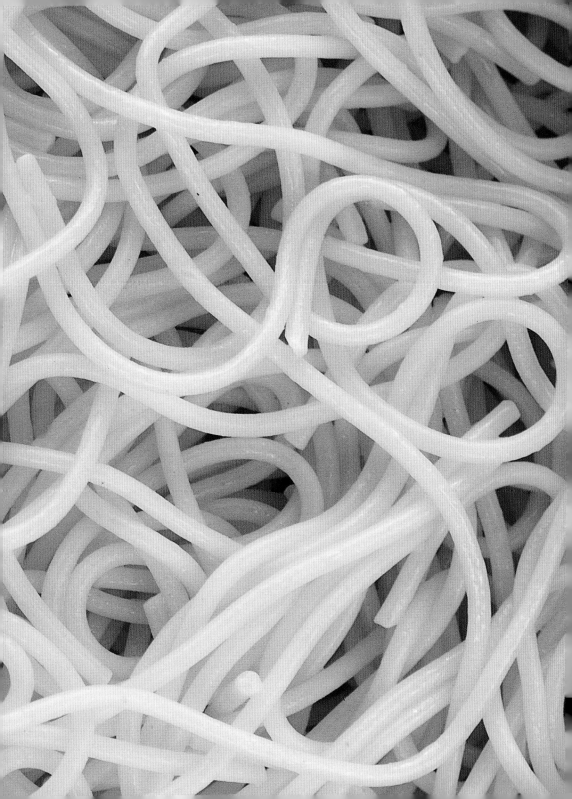

Pasta with chilli pesto

1 large red pepper
50g/2oz fresh basil leaves
1 garlic clove, crushed
2 ripe tomatoes, skinned
2 tbsp pine nuts
3 tbsp sun-dried tomato paste
3 tbsp tomato purée

1 tsp mild chilli powder
few drops of Tabasco sauce
50g/2oz Parmesan cheese, freshly
   grated
150ml/¼ pint light olive oil
450g/1lb dried caserecce or spaghetti

1 Grill the red pepper, turning occasionally, until charred. Cool slightly, then skin, halve and de-seed. Place in a food processor with the other ingredients, except the oil and pasta. Work until almost smooth. Turn into a bowl and stir in the oil.

2 Bring a large pan of salted water to the boil. Then add the pasta and cook until al dente.

3 Drain the pasta, keeping back 2 tbsp water in the pan. Immediately toss with chilli pesto to taste, allowing approximately 2 tbsp per serving.

Note Store any leftover pesto in a jar, covered with a layer of olive oil, in the fridge for up to 2 weeks. It is excellent with grilled chicken.

This robust pasta dish is spiked with a fiery homemade chilli pesto – to delicious effect.

Fusilli with tomatoes and mozzarella

500g/1lb 2oz plum tomatoes, roughly chopped
1 garlic clove, crushed
2 tbsp chopped fresh basil
2 tsp chopped fresh marjoram
4 anchovy fillets, finely chopped

juice of ½ lemon
4 tbsp extra virgin olive oil
salt and pepper
450g/1lb dried tricolore fusilli or pasta shells
350g/12oz mozzarella cheese, diced

1 Place the chopped tomatoes, garlic, herbs, anchovies, lemon juice and olive oil in a bowl. Season with pepper and a little salt, toss to mix and set aside.
2 Cook the pasta in a large pan of boiling salted water until al dente.
3 Drain the pasta and place in a warm serving bowl. Immediately add the mozzarella and toss to melt slightly, then add the tomato sauce and toss well. Check the seasoning and serve at once.

Tricolore pasta with a sauce of plum tomatoes, marjoram, basil, anchovies and mozzarella.

Fettuccine with vegetable julienne

600ml/1 pint homemade or bought fresh chicken stock
200g/7oz carrots, cut into julienne strips
200g/7oz leek, cut into julienne strips

3 tomatoes, skinned, seeded and sliced
pepper
300g/10oz dried fettuccine or tagliatelle
freshly grated Parmesan, to serve

1 Bring the chicken stock to the boil in a pan. Add the carrots and simmer for about 2 minutes; remove with a slotted spoon and place in a bowl. Repeat with the leeks; add to the bowl. Boil the stock to reduce by about half.
2 Cook the pasta in a large pan of boiling salted water until al dente.
3 Add the leeks, carrots and tomatoes to the chicken stock and bring to a simmer to warm through.
4 Drain the pasta and add to the vegetable julienne and stock. Serve in warmed bowls.

For this delicately flavoured pasta dish, vegetable julienne are cooked briefly in a tasty stock, then combined with noodles.

Fusilli with fennel and red onion

Illustrated on previous pages

1 fennel bulb, trimmed, cored and
  finely diced
500g/1lb 2oz ripe plum tomatoes,
  seeded and finely diced
1 red onion, finely diced
2 tbsp chopped fresh basil
2 tbsp chopped fresh dill
3 tbsp extra virgin olive oil

juice of 1 lemon
salt and pepper
450g/1lb dried fusilli (preferably
  corn pasta)
basil leaves and red onion slices,
  to garnish
freshly grated Parmesan cheese,
  to serve

1 In a bowl, mix together the fennel, tomatoes, red onion, herbs, olive
oil and lemon juice. Season with salt and pepper to taste and set aside.
2 Cook the pasta in a large pan of boiling salted water until al dente.
3 Drain the pasta, and return to the pan. Add the fennel sauce and toss
to mix. Check the seasoning. Cover with a lid and then leave to stand
for 2-3 minutes to allow the flavours to infuse.
4 Serve garnished with basil and red onion slices. Accompany with some
grated Parmesan.

Fresh fennel, dill, red onion, tomatoes and
herbs give this uncooked sauce a wonderfully
refreshing taste sensation.

Spaghetti with aubergines

Serves 4-6

900g/2lb aubergines, cut into
  1cm/½in dice
salt and pepper
5 tbsp olive oil
2-3 tbsp crushed sun-dried tomatoes
  in oil
1 tbsp finely shredded fresh basil
  leaves
500g/1lb 2oz dried spaghetti
75g/2½oz pine nuts, toasted
freshly grated pecorino or Parmesan
  cheese, to serve

1 Put the aubergines in a colander and sprinkle generously with salt.
Leave to drain for 30 minutes. Rinse well and pat dry on a tea towel.
2 Heat the oil in a pan and fry the aubergines for about 15 minutes, until
tender and brown. Add the sun-dried tomatoes, basil and pepper.
3 Meanwhile, cook the spaghetti in a large pan of boiling salted water until
al dente. Drain and toss with the aubergine mixture and pine nuts. Serve
at once, with grated pecorino or Parmesan.

Note It is worth salting the aubergines for this dish, to draw out their
bitter juices.

Spaghetti tossed with a rustic sauce of fried
aubergine, crushed sun-dried tomato and
toasted pine nuts. Serve with a rocket salad.

Pasta with courgettes and mushrooms

450g/1lb dried curly pasta shapes,
   such as spiralli or caserecce, or
   shells
salt and pepper
50g/2oz butter
1 garlic clove, chopped

4-6 large flat mushrooms, sliced
1 tbsp chopped fresh thyme
4 small courgettes, coarsely grated
pecorino or Parmesan cheese
   shavings, to serve

1 Bring a large pan of salted water to the boil. Add the pasta and cook until al dente.

2 Meanwhile, melt the butter in a frying pan. Add the garlic and cook gently for 2-3 minutes until golden.

3 Add the sliced mushrooms and fry for about 2 minutes until softened and beginning to brown.

4 Stir in the thyme and grated courgettes. Increase the heat and cook, stirring constantly, for about 5 minutes or until the courgettes are tender. Season with salt and pepper to taste.

5 Drain the pasta, keeping 2 tbsp water in the pan. Immediately toss the pasta with the sauce and serve topped with pecorino or Parmesan shavings.

Note For speed, use a food processor fitted with a coarse grating disc to prepare the courgettes, or dice them if you prefer.

Variation Use 175g (6oz) button or chestnut mushrooms instead of flat mushrooms.

Mushrooms and courgettes are perfect partners. Sautéed with garlic and thyme, they make a wonderful aromatic sauce.

Spaghetti with garlic crumbs and broccoli

50g/2oz butter
2 garlic cloves, crushed
50g/2oz fresh white breadcrumbs
300g/10oz broccoli, divided into
   sprigs
salt and pepper
225g/8oz dried spaghetti

6 tbsp extra virgin olive oil
1 red chilli, seeded and diced
juice of ½ lemon
1 tbsp chopped fresh parsley
freshly grated Parmesan cheese,
   to serve

1 Melt the butter in a large frying pan. Add the garlic and breadcrumbs and stir-fry over a medium heat until golden. Remove and set aside.
2 Blanch the broccoli in boiling water for 2 minutes; drain and refresh under cold water.
3 Add the spaghetti to a large pan of boiling salted water and then cook until al dente.
4 Meanwhile, heat half the oil in a clean frying pan, add the chilli and broccoli and stir-fry for 3 minutes until tender. Add the lemon juice, remaining oil and parsley.
5 Drain the spaghetti, retaining 4 tbsp cooking water. Add to the broccoli and toss over a low heat for 1 minute. Serve topped with the garlic breadcrumbs and a little grated Parmesan.

Sprouting broccoli is ideal for this simple pasta dish. Otherwise you can use calabrese, cavolo nero or spring greens.

Spaghetti with leeks and pancetta

Serves 4-6

2 tbsp olive oil

2 medium leeks, thinly sliced

175g/6oz pancetta, thinly sliced

100ml/3½fl oz white wine

300ml/½ pint single cream

500g/1lb 2oz dried spaghetti

3 tbsp freshly grated Parmesan
  cheese

1 Heat the oil in a pan and fry the leeks gently for 3-4 minutes to soften. Add the pancetta and cook for 4-5 minutes until beginning to brown.

2 Add the wine, stir to deglaze, and bring nearly to the boil. Add the cream and warm through.

3 Meanwhile, cook the spaghetti in a large pan of boiling salted water until al dente. Drain and toss with the sauce and Parmesan to serve.

This deliciously rich, creamy dish is equally good with tagliatelle or linguine.

Spaghetti with pepper butter sauce

3 large red peppers
250g/9oz dried spaghetti
salt and pepper
85g/3oz butter
dash of Tabasco sauce
2 tbsp chopped fresh basil

4 tbsp milk
shredded basil leaves, to garnish
freshly grated Parmesan cheese,
   to serve

1 Peel the red peppers, using a potato peeler, then halve and remove the core
and seeds. Place the pepper flesh in a food processor and work to a purée.
2 Cook the spaghetti in a large pan of boiling salted water until al dente.
3 Meanwhile, transfer the red pepper purée to a saucepan and add the butter,
Tabasco, chopped basil and milk. Season generously with salt and pepper.
Cover and simmer gently, stirring frequently, for 8-10 minutes.
4 Drain the spaghetti and return to the warm pan. Add the pepper butter
sauce and toss to mix.
5 Divide the pasta between warmed serving plates. Sprinkle with basil and
serve with grated Parmesan.

Freshly puréed peppers give this sauce a silky
texture and sweet flavour, while Tabasco adds
a touch of heat. Serve with a rocket salad.

Spinach tagliatelle with minted peas

450g/1lb dried spinach tagliatelle
salt and pepper
85g/3oz butter
4 spring onions, thinly sliced
550g/1¼lb peas (shelled fresh or
   frozen)

2 tbsp chopped fresh mint
2 tsp finely grated orange rind
1 tbsp orange juice
freshly grated Parmesan cheese,
   to serve

1 Cook the tagliatelle in a large pan of boiling salted water until al dente.
2 Meanwhile, melt 50g/2oz of the butter in a pan. Add the spring onions and cook gently for 3-4 minutes or until tender.
3 Add the peas and 100ml/3½fl oz water; cook for 3-4 minutes or until tender. Stir in the mint.
4 Put the remaining butter, orange rind and juice in a large, warm serving dish. Drain the pasta and add to the dish with the pea sauce. Toss well and season with salt and pepper to taste.
5 Serve topped with grated Parmesan.

Spinach tagliatelle with spring onions, peas and chopped mint in an orange butter sauce.

Pasta with avocado and coriander pesto

2 small, ripe avocados
3 spring onions, finely chopped
50g/2oz fresh coriander leaves
1 tbsp lime juice
few drops of Jalapeno or Tabasco
 sauce

2 tbsp crème fraîche
1 large tomato, skinned and diced
salt and pepper
450g/1lb dried buckwheat noodles,
 or wholewheat spaghetti
coriander leaves, to garnish

1 Halve, stone and peel the avocados. Put them in a food processor with the spring onions, coriander leaves, lime juice and Jalapeno or Tabasco sauce. Pulse until the ingredients are evenly mixed and finely chopped.
2 Turn into a bowl and stir in the crème fraîche, then the diced tomato. Season with salt and pepper to taste.
3 Bring a large pan of salted water to the boil. Add the noodles or spaghetti and cook until al dente.
4 Drain the pasta, keeping back 2 tbsp water in the pan. Immediately toss with the sauce and serve scattered with coriander leaves.

Note In general, chunky sauces are best with chunky pasta, such as spirals, penne, shells or rigatoni. Soft, fluid sauces suit long pasta, like noodles or spaghetti.

This wonderfully pungent pesto sauce is particularly good with buckwheat noodles.

Penne with roasted beetroot and feta

450g/1lb baby beetroot, trimmed
  (see note)
1 garlic clove, crushed
2 tbsp walnut oil, plus extra to
  drizzle
salt and pepper
300g/10oz dried penne or other
  pasta shapes

50g/2oz rocket leaves
100g/4oz feta cheese, crumbled
2 tbsp toasted pine nuts
pecorino or Parmesan cheese,
  to serve

1 Preheat oven to 220C/fan oven 200C/Gas 7. Put the beetroot in a small roasting tin with the garlic, oil, salt and pepper. Add 2 tbsp water and roast in the oven for 50-60 minutes until tender. Keep warm.

2 Cook the pasta in a large pan of boiling salted water until al dente.

3 Drain the pasta thoroughly and immediately toss with the rocket leaves, roasted beetroot, pepper and a little extra walnut oil.

4 Spoon the pasta mixture into warmed bowls and scatter over the crumbled feta and toasted pine nuts. Drizzle with walnut oil to serve.

Note To ensure the baby beets are similar in size, halve any larger ones.

Sweet roasted beetroot and salty feta combine well in this pretty pasta dish. The rocket just wilts as it is stirred into the hot pasta.

Tomato spaghetti with coriander and avocado

Illustrated on previous pages

500g/1lb 2oz cherry tomatoes, quartered
2 tbsp torn fresh coriander leaves
grated rind and juice of ½ lemon
1 garlic clove, crushed
3 tbsp extra virgin olive oil

3 small avocados (preferably hass), peeled, stoned and cut into 1cm/½in dice
salt and pepper
450g/1lb dried tomato spaghetti

1 Combine the tomatoes, coriander, lemon rind and juice, garlic and olive oil in a large bowl. Add the diced avocados and toss gently to mix. Season with salt and pepper to taste and set aside.
2 Cook the pasta in a large pan of boiling salted water until al dente.
3 Drain the pasta and toss gently with the sauce to serve.

Note Don't prepare this sauce too far in advance, or the avocado may discolour and spoil the appearance of the dish.

The heat of the cooked spaghetti brings out the full flavours of creamy, ripe avocados and cherry tomatoes.

Buckwheat noodles with Savoy cabbage

2 tbsp olive oil
125g/4½oz pancetta or lightly
  smoked bacon, diced
2 red onions, sliced
225g/8oz Savoy cabbage, shredded
3 garlic cloves, chopped

225g/8oz buckwheat (soba) noodles,
  or egg tagliatelle
salt and pepper
250g tub mascarpone cheese
140g/5oz dolcelatte cheese, diced

1 Heat the oil in a large deep frying pan, add the pancetta or bacon and onions and fry for 5 minutes, stirring occasionally.
2 Stir in the cabbage and garlic, cover and cook for 8-10 minutes until the cabbage is tender.
3 Meanwhile, cook the noodles in a large pan of boiling salted water until al dente.
4 Drain the noodles thoroughly and toss with the cabbage; season. Add the cheeses and heat gently until they melt to a creamy sauce. Serve immediately.

Japanese noodles tossed with pancetta and cabbage in a creamy cheese sauce.

Spaghetti, peas and oven-dried tomatoes

Serves 4-6
500g/1lb 2oz dried spaghetti
salt and pepper
450g/1lb frozen or fresh peas or
  petits pois

1 batch oven-dried tomatoes
  (see below)
2 tbsp finely shredded fresh mint

1 Cook the spaghetti in a large pan of boiling salted water until al dente.
2 Meanwhile, cook the peas in a separate pan of boiling water until tender.
3 Drain the pasta and peas, return to the warm pasta pan and add the oven-dried tomatoes with 2-3 tbsp of the oil, and the mint. Toss lightly, season and serve.

Oven-dried tomatoes Preheat oven to 130C/fan oven 110C/Gas 1. Lay 400g/14oz halved cherry tomatoes on a non-stick baking tray cut-side up. Sprinkle with salt, pepper and sugar. Bake for 1½ hours or until dry but not brown. Cool slightly, then put into a bowl and add extra virgin olive oil to cover. When cold, store in jars covered with a layer of olive oil. Use as required.

Oven-dried cherry tomatoes bring a sweet intensity to this dish.

Tagliatelle with wild mushroom sauce

20g/¾oz dried porcini mushrooms
150ml/¼ pint dry white wine
3 garlic cloves, peeled
300ml/½ pint double cream
50g/2oz walnuts
2 tbsp olive oil
400g/14oz mixed oyster, chestnut
  and wild or field mushrooms,
  halved if large

salt and pepper
375g/13oz dried egg tagliatelle
cep powder, to sprinkle (optional,
  see note)
chervil sprigs, to garnish

1 Soak the dried porcini in the wine for 30 minutes to soften. Strain the soaking liquid into a small heavy-based pan, squeezing out all excess liquid from the porcini.

2 Add the garlic to the pan and simmer until softened and the liquid is reduced by half; take out the garlic and set aside. Stir the cream into the liquid; remove from the heat.

3 Chop the garlic, nuts and porcini together, to a coarse paste. Heat the oil in a wok or deep frying pan and stir-fry the mushrooms over a high heat, adding firmer ones first. Season well. Lower the heat and stir in the walnut paste, then the sauce; heat through.

4 Add the tagliatelle to a large pan of boiling salted water and cook until al dente. Drain well and toss the pasta with the mushroom sauce. Serve dusted with cep powder if wished, and scattered with chervil.

Note Cep powder adds a special finishing touch. It is available in a shaker from larger supermarkets or, to make your own, grind dried ceps to a powder in a coffee grinder.

Locate a good selection of mushrooms, including wild ones if possible. Use mushroom flavoured tagliatelle if preferred.

Pasta with bacon and wilted spinach

450g/1lb dried spaghetti, tagliatelle
  or linguine
salt and pepper
4 tbsp olive oil
8 slices pancetta or unsmoked
  streaky bacon, chopped

2 garlic cloves, finely chopped
900g/2lb spinach leaves, stalks
  removed
150ml/¼ pint double cream
freshly grated nutmeg
3 tbsp pine nuts, toasted

1 Bring a large pan of salted water to the boil. Add the pasta and cook until al dente.

2 Meanwhile heat the oil in a large pan, add the pancetta or bacon and fry until just turning golden. Add the garlic and cook for 1 minute.

3 Stir in the spinach and cook over a high heat for a few minutes or until the leaves are just wilted. Pour in the cream, turning the spinach to ensure it is well coated. Season with salt, pepper and nutmeg. Heat until boiling.

4 Drain the pasta, keeping back 2 tbsp water in the pan. Immediately toss the pasta with the hot sauce. Serve sprinkled with the pine nuts.

Bacon, garlic and spinach are mellowed in a cream sauce. Don't overcook the fresh spinach – it should be vivid green and full of flavour.

Pasta with tuna tapenade

175g/6oz black olives (preferably Greek), stoned

2 tbsp capers in brine, rinsed

10 canned anchovy fillets in oil, drained

125g/4½oz canned tuna fish in oil, drained

100ml/3½fl oz olive oil

1 canned red pepper (capsicum), rinsed, seeded and diced

2 tbsp chopped fresh basil

lemon juice, to taste

salt and pepper

450g/1lb dried pasta shapes, such as ballerine, radiattore, caserecce, capelletti

1 Chop the olives, capers, anchovies and tuna in a food processor.

2 With the motor running, add the oil in a steady stream and mix briefly.

3 Transfer to a bowl and stir in the diced pepper and chopped basil. Flavour with lemon juice and season with salt and pepper to taste.

4 Bring a large pan of salted water to the boil. Add the pasta and cook until al dente. Drain, keeping 2 tbsp water in the pan. Immediately toss the pasta with the sauce. Cover and leave to stand for 2-3 minutes before serving.

Tuna tapenade is an easy no-cook sauce for pasta. It relies on the heat of the cooked pasta to warm the ingredients.

Pasta with Mediterranean sauce

175g/6oz soft fresh goat's cheese
2 tbsp capers in vinegar, drained
225g/8oz mixed green and black
   olives, stoned and chopped
8 sun-dried tomatoes in oil, drained
   and chopped

1 tsp dried oregano (preferably
   freeze-dried)
salt and pepper
450g/1lb dried pasta shapes, such as
   ballerine, radiattore, caserecce,
   capelletti

1 In a bowl, mix the goat's cheese with the capers, olives, sun-dried tomatoes, oregano and seasoning to taste.
2 Cook the pasta in a large pan of salted water until al dente. Drain, keeping back 2 tbsp water in the pan. Immediately toss the pasta with the sauce. Cover and leave to stand for 3 minutes before serving.

Sun-dried tomatoes, capers, olives and goat's cheese make a delicious no-cook sauce. The heat of the pasta melts the cheese to make a creamy sauce.

Rigatoni with cherry tomato and basil sauce

450g/1lb ripe cherry tomatoes,
   quartered
2 garlic cloves, finely chopped
4 tbsp shredded fresh basil
150ml/¼ pint extra virgin olive oil
salt and pepper

450g/1lb dried chunky pasta
   shapes, such as rigatoni, penne,
   farfalle
100g/4oz feta cheese, thinly sliced

1 In a bowl, mix the tomatoes with the garlic, basil, olive oil and seasoning. Cover and leave to infuse for at least 30 minutes; do not refrigerate.
2 Bring a large pan of salted water to the boil. Add the pasta and cook until al dente. Drain, keeping back 2 tbsp water in the pan. Immediately toss the pasta with the sauce. Cover with a lid and leave to stand for 3 minutes.
3 Remove the lid, stir and serve topped with slices of feta.

A wonderfully fresh tasting pasta dish. Marinating the tomatoes with the garlic and basil is important to develop the flavours.

Pasta with garlic and anchovy sauce

3 tbsp olive oil
3 garlic cloves, chopped
1 small can anchovies in oil, drained
 and chopped
400g can chopped tomatoes

pepper
450g/1lb dried bucatini, macaroni or
 pasta shapes
10 large fresh basil leaves, shredded
100g/4oz fresh rocket leaves

1 Heat the olive oil in a saucepan. Add the garlic and fry until just colouring. Stir in the anchovies and cook gently until they begin to dissolve.
2 Stir in the chopped tomatoes and bring to the boil. Season to taste with pepper (salt won't be needed as the anchovies are quite salty). Cover and simmer gently for 10 minutes.
3 Meanwhile, bring a large pan of salted water to the boil. Add the pasta and cook until al dente. Drain the pasta, keeping back 2 tbsp water in the pan.
4 Stir the shredded basil into the tomato and anchovy sauce. Immediately add to the pasta and toss well. Serve each portion topped with a tangle of rocket leaves.

Pasta in a classic tomato sauce infused with the savoury saltiness of melted anchovies, topped with contrasting peppery rocket.

Smoked haddock frittata

Illustrated on previous pages

40g/1½oz butter
300g/10oz skinless smoked haddock
   fillet
8 large eggs
4 tbsp milk
salt and pepper
2 tbsp finely chopped spring onion

2 tbsp snipped chives
85g/3oz cooked pasta twists or shells
   (ie. 25g/1oz dried weight)
100g/4oz mature Churnton or
   Cheddar cheese, grated
snipped chives, to garnish

1 Heat half the butter in a large frying pan. Add the smoked haddock, cover tightly and cook for 3 minutes. Lift out of the pan and flake roughly.
2 Beat the eggs with the milk, seasoning, spring onion, chives and the cooked pasta. Preheat the grill.
3 Melt the remaining butter in the frying pan, then pour in the egg mixture and scatter over half of the flaked fish. Move the mixture round the pan with a wooden spatula until half set.
4 Remove from the heat and top with the remaining smoked haddock. Sprinkle with the cheese and extra chives. Grill for about 2 minutes until set and puffy. Serve with a salad and crusty bread.

Note Make sure you use a cast-iron pan or other frying pan which is suitable for placing under the grill.

Variation Replace the smoked haddock with a 200g/7oz packet of wafer-thin smoked ham. Scrunch up the ham and scatter over the frittata before sprinkling with cheese.

Smoked haddock, mellow cheese and a hint of onion give this omelette a wonderful flavour, while the pasta makes it more substantial.

Farfalle with potted shrimp

Serves 1

85g/3oz dried farfalle or other pasta
  shapes
salt and pepper
55g tub potted shrimps (see note)
freshly grated nutmeg (optional)
1 tbsp finely chopped fresh parsley

1 Cook the pasta in a large pan of boiling salted water until al dente.
2 Drain the pasta, return to the pan and toss in the shrimps with their butter. Warm through until the butter melts.
3 Add grated nutmeg to taste, toss in the chopped parsley and serve.

Note Potted shrimps are packed in butter flavoured with cayenne, nutmeg and mace. For additional spice, add extra nutmeg.

This simple dish is an ideal speedy supper for one. Accompany with a tomato and avocado salad, and warm bread.

Macaroni bakes with balsamic vinegar

100g/4oz dried elbow macaroni
salt and pepper
300ml/½ pint double cream
50g/2oz gruyère cheese, grated
25g/1oz Parmesan cheese, freshly
  grated
3 eggs, beaten

For the dressing
1 shallot, finely diced
2 ripe tomatoes, peeled, seeded and
  diced
6 tbsp extra virgin olive oil
few fresh thyme leaves
1 tbsp balsamic vinegar

1 Preheat oven to 180C/fan oven 160C/Gas 4. Oil and base line 4 timbales or ovenproof cups.

2 Cook the pasta in boiling salted water until al dente. Drain thoroughly and divide between the timbales or cups.

3 Slowly bring the cream to the boil in a pan. Remove from the heat, season and stir in the cheeses until melted. Stir into the beaten eggs. Pour the savoury custard over the macaroni.

4 Stand the moulds in a roasting tin, half filled with boiling water. Bake for 25 minutes.

5 Remove the moulds from the bain-marie; let rest for 5 minutes. Warm the dressing ingredients together in a small pan for 5 minutes or until the shallots are softened; season with salt and pepper to taste.

6 Turn out the pasta moulds onto warmed plates and surround with the tomato dressing. Garnish with thyme to serve.

Macaroni baked in a savoury cheese custard in timbales, then turned out and served with a piquant tomato sauce.

easy
fish

Peppered salmon with juniper and vermouth

1 tsp dried green peppercorns
16 juniper berries
1 tsp salt
4 salmon steaks or fillets, skinned
25g/1oz unsalted butter

8 tbsp dry vermouth (preferably
  Noilly Prat)
2-3 tbsp double cream or crème
  fraîche

1 Crush together the peppercorns, juniper berries and salt, using a pestle and mortar (or end of a rolling pin and strong bowl). Sprinkle over the salmon and press well to adhere.
2 Melt the butter in a frying pan over a medium heat and fry the seasoned fish for about 10-12 minutes for steaks, a little less for salmon fillets, turning once.
3 Lift the salmon onto a warm serving dish; keep warm while you finish the sauce.
4 Deglaze the pan with the vermouth and let bubble for 2-3 minutes until syrupy. Stir in the cream or crème fraîche and let bubble for 2 minutes. Spoon the sauce over the salmon to serve.

Note If buying salmon by the piece to cut into portions, choose the middle or tail end as this is less oily than the head end.

An easy dish with intriguing flavours –
delicious with herby mashed potatoes.

Basque baked fish in parchment

Illustrated on previous pages

4 cod or haddock fillets, each
   175-200g/6-7oz, skinned
½ green pepper, cored, seeded and
   diced
½ red pepper, cored, seeded and diced
1 onion, finely chopped
1 tbsp fresh oregano leaves, chopped
2 garlic cloves, finely chopped

2 plum tomatoes, skinned, seeded
   and chopped
juice of 1 lemon
1 tbsp olive oil
4 tbsp dry white wine
salt and pepper
12 black olives (optional)

1 Preheat oven to 190C/fan oven 170C/Gas 5. Cut 4 sheets of non-stick
baking parchment, measuring approximately 30x38cm/12x15in. Place
each fish fillet on a piece of paper, positioning it slightly off centre.
2 In a bowl, mix together the peppers, onion, oregano, garlic, tomatoes,
lemon juice, olive oil and wine. Season with salt and pepper.
3 Spoon the mixture on top of the fish and scatter over the olives, if using.
Fold the parchment over the fish to form a triangle. Fold the edges together
tightly to form a sealed parcel.
4 Lift the parcels onto a baking sheet and bake for 15-20 minutes until the
fish is cooked through. Place each parcel on a warmed plate and serve at
once, with buttery new potatoes and steamed broccoli.

These fish parcels cook quickly and easily
in the oven, trapping in the flavours of sweet
peppers, onion, garlic and oregano.

Portuguese fish and potato bake

750g/1lb 10oz thick cod fillets,
  skinned
5 tbsp olive oil
3 large onions, halved and thinly
  sliced
3 garlic cloves, finely chopped
600g/1lb 5oz potatoes (King Edward
  or Desiree)

3 tbsp finely chopped fresh parsley
16 black olives, stoned and roughly
  chopped
salt and pepper
150ml/¼ pint fish or chicken stock
For the garnish
4 hard-boiled eggs, quartered
chopped flat leaf parsley

1 Preheat oven to 180C/fan oven 160C/Gas 4. Place the fish fillets on
a lightly oiled baking sheet, brush with olive oil and bake for 7-10 minutes.
Let cool slightly.

2 Meanwhile, heat the remaining oil in a large frying pan, add the onions
and sauté for about 20 minutes until golden brown. Add the garlic and sauté
for 2 minutes; set aside.

3 In the meantime, boil the potatoes until tender. Drain and leave to cool
slightly, then peel and cut into 1cm/½in slices.

4 When the fish is cool enough to handle, separate into large flakes.

5 Lightly oil a shallow ovenproof dish, 24-25cm/9½-10in in diameter. Layer
the potatoes, onions, parsley, olives and fish in the dish, seasoning each
layer generously and finishing with a layer of onions. Pour in the stock and
bake for 20 minutes.

6 Serve garnished with hard-boiled eggs and chopped parsley. Accompany
with green beans or roasted tomatoes.

Flavoured with caramelised onions, black
olives and garlic, this tasty bake is best
enjoyed with a glass of rioja.

Warm smoked haddock and butter bean salad

4 small cooked beetroot, diced
2 tsp cider vinegar
500g/1lb 2oz undyed smoked
   haddock fillet, skinned
1 bunch watercress, trimmed

400g can butter beans, drained
3 spring onions, finely sliced
pepper

1 Toss the diced beetroot in the cider vinegar; set aside.
2 Poach the haddock in just sufficient water to cover for 4-5 minutes until opaque; drain.
3 Meanwhile gently mix the watercress sprigs, butter beans, onions and beetroot together in a shallow serving bowl.
4 When the fish is cool enough to handle, divide into flakes and scatter over the salad. Season with plenty of pepper.

Note The beetroot lightly tinges the beans a pretty pale pink. Combine the salad shortly before serving to avoid over-colouring.

Smokey haddock marries with sweet beetroot and creamy butter beans to make a satisfying meal that is low in fat.

Tagliatelle, smoked salmon and pesto

Illustrated on previous pages

100g/4oz blanched whole almonds
1 garlic clove, finely chopped
2 tbsp freshly grated Parmesan
  cheese
50g/2oz fresh parsley leaves,
  roughly chopped
150ml/¼ pint light olive oil

2 tbsp curd cheese
salt and pepper
500g/1lb 2oz dried tagliatelle
225g/8oz sliced smoked salmon, cut
  into strips
flat leaf parsley, to garnish

1 Spread the almonds on a baking sheet and place under the grill for
1-2 minutes, turning frequently, until toasted and golden. Allow to cool,
then chop roughly. Beat together with the garlic, Parmesan, parsley, olive
oil and curd cheese. Season with salt and pepper to taste.
2 Add the tagliatelle to a large pan of boiling salted water and cook
according to the packet directions until al dente (cooked, but still firm
to the bite). Drain, keeping back 2-3 tbsp of the cooking water.
3 Add the parsley pesto to the pasta and toss well to mix. Pile into warmed
bowls and top each serving with a tangle of smoked salmon. Garnish with
flat leaf parsley and serve at once.

Note Don't be tempted to whizz the pesto ingredients in a food processor
until smooth. A coarse textured pesto gives a better result for this recipe.

Tagliatelle is tossed with a coarse pesto of
toasted almonds, garlic, parsley, Parmesan and
olive oil, then topped with smoked salmon.

Salmon and potato slice

700g/1lb 9oz potatoes, skin on,
  thinly sliced
85g/3oz butter, melted
1 tsp celery or fennel seeds
salt and pepper

700g/1lb 9oz skinless salmon fillet
  (tail end)
3 tbsp single cream
chopped flat leaf parsley, to garnish

1 Preheat oven to 200C/fan oven 180C/Gas 6. Parcook the potatoes in water
or stock for 4-5 minutes; the slices must remain whole. Drain and refresh
under cold water; drain.

2 Line a buttered shallow 18x25cm/7x10in ovenproof dish with half of the
potatoes, brushing with butter and sprinkling with celery or fennel seed,
salt and pepper.

3 Cut the fish into chunks and lay over the potato; season and drizzle over
the cream. Top with the remaining potato, seasoning as before. Bake for
40 minutes until the topping is crisp. Garnish with parsley.

Salmon fillet is baked between layers of potato
and celery seed, keeping it moist, while the
potato topping becomes crisp.

Crab and papaya salad

Illustrated on previous pages

Serves 3-4

350g/12oz fresh white crab meat
(see note)

2 ripe tomatoes, skinned, seeded
and diced

1 red chilli, seeded and finely
chopped

2 tbsp chopped fresh coriander
leaves

2 tbsp extra virgin olive oil

3 tbsp lime juice

few drops of Tabasco sauce

1 small papaya

salt and pepper

2 trevise or chicory bulbs

a little extra virgin olive oil

squeeze of lime juice

coriander leaves and lime wedges,
to garnish

1 Carefully pick over the crab meat, discarding any small pieces of shell
or cartilage, then place in a bowl.

2 Stir in the tomatoes, chilli, coriander, olive oil, lime juice and Tabasco
sauce. Cover and leave to infuse in the refrigerator for at least 1 hour.

3 Just before serving, peel the papaya and scoop out the seeds. Dice the
papaya flesh and stir into the crab meat. Check the seasoning.

4 Separate the trevise or chicory leaves and dress with a little olive oil and
lime juice. Arrange on individual serving plates. Spoon the crab salad on top
and garnish with coriander leaves. Serve immediately, with lime wedges and
warm French bread.

Note If you prefer to buy a whole crab, choose one that weighs at least
1.5kg/3lb to obtain the required amount of white meat.

Either buy a freshly dressed crab or use
vacuum packed fresh crab meat for this tangy
crab salad.

Potted crab with ginger and garlic

4 small dressed crabs, each about
    200g/7oz
100g/4oz unsalted butter
1cm/¾in piece fresh root ginger,
    peeled and grated

1 garlic clove, crushed
1 tsp sweet paprika
salt and pepper

1 Scoop the meat out of the crab shells, discarding any fragments of shell.
2 Melt the butter slowly in a small saucepan. Add the ginger and garlic and
cook over a gentle heat for 3-5 minutes until soft but not coloured.
3 Add the paprika and crab. Stir to coat with the butter and heat through;
season with salt and pepper to taste.
4 Spoon the crab mixture into small pots or ramekins and smooth the tops.
Allow to cool, then chill in the refrigerator for at least 1 hour to set.
5 Serve the potted crab with warm toasted pitta bread fingers.

Note Small ready prepared fresh crabs are obtainable from most
supermarket fresh fish counters.

Fresh, ready prepared crab mixed with a
spiced clarified butter and set in little pots.
Serve with warm, toasted pitta bread.

Smoked mackerel and spinach frittata

Illustrated on previous pages

Serves 3-4

450g/1lb ready-prepared young
   fresh spinach
2 tbsp olive oil
225g/8oz smoked mackerel fillets
175g/6oz small new potatoes
salt and pepper
100g/4oz butter
6 large eggs
50g/2oz Parmesan cheese, freshly
   grated

1 Remove any tough stems from the spinach. Heat the oil in a frying pan, add the spinach and toss until just wilted; transfer to a plate. Remove the skin from the mackerel fillets and roughly flake the flesh.

2 Cook the potatoes in boiling salted water for 15-20 minutes until just tender. Drain and allow to cool slightly, then slice thickly.

3 Heat half the butter in a non-stick frying pan and sauté the potatoes for 5 minutes or until beginning to colour.

4 In a bowl, beat the eggs with half of the Parmesan, a good pinch of salt and plenty of pepper. Stir in the spinach and potatoes.

5 Melt the remaining butter in a 25cm/10in heavy non-stick frying pan. When foaming, pour in the egg mixture. Turn down the heat as low as possible. Cook for about 15 minutes until set, with the top still a little runny. Scatter over the flaked mackerel and sprinkle with the remaining Parmesan.

6 Place briefly under a hot grill to lightly brown the cheese and just set the top; do not overbrown or the frittata will dry out. Slide onto a warm plate and cut into wedges. Serve with a crisp salad.

This Italian omelette is cooked slowly and the filling is stirred into the eggs or scattered on top. A frittata is served just set, never folded.

Pan-fried monkfish with Dijon mustard

40g/1½oz unsalted butter
2 monkfish fillets, each about
    300g/10oz, skinned and thickly
    sliced
1 garlic clove, crushed

100ml/3½fl oz extra dry white
    vermouth
1 tbsp Dijon mustard
150ml/¼ pint double cream
1 tbsp snipped fresh chives (optional)

1 Melt the butter in a large frying pan and briefly fry the monkfish for
1-2 minutes until almost cooked. Lift from the pan.
2 Add the garlic to the pan and fry gently until softened. Add the vermouth
and mustard and bubble vigorously to boil off the alcohol.
3 Stir in the cream, and chives if using, then return the fish to the pan
to warm through and finish cooking. Serve with tagliatelle and sugar snap
peas or mangetout.

Flash-fried monkfish slices in a creamy
mustard sauce with a dash of vermouth.

Herring with mustard lemon butter

100g/4oz pinhead oatmeal
grated rind and juice of 1 lemon
4 large herring fillets
100ml/3½fl oz milk
50g/2oz butter

1 lemon, thinly sliced
1 tbsp wholegrain mustard
2 tbsp chopped fresh parsley
salt and pepper

1 Mix the oatmeal with the lemon rind. Dip the herring into the milk, then into the oatmeal to coat on both sides.
2 Melt the butter in a large frying pan and fry the herring fillets with the lemon slices for about 2 minutes on each side; transfer to warm plates and keep warm.
3 Add the lemon juice, mustard and parsley to the pan and heat until bubbling; season. Pour over the herring and serve.

Fillets of herring are dipped in oatmeal mixed with grated lemon rind, then pan-fried in butter flavoured with lemon and parsley.

Salmon baguette

Serves 2

1 baguette, about 5cm/2in across,
    22cm/8-9in in length,
4-6 tbsp pesto
250g/9oz fresh salmon fillet
pepper

1 Preheat oven to 220C/fan oven 200C/Gas 7. Split a baguette, without cutting right through. Spread both cut faces with pesto.
2 Finely slice the fresh salmon fillet into 5mm/¼in slices. Fill the baguette with the salmon, overlapping the slices, and season with pepper.
3 Wrap the baguette in oiled foil and bake for about 30 minutes. Open the foil slightly to let out steam and then return to the oven for a few minutes. Cut the baguette in half and serve in napkins.

An original meal for two. Simply split a baguette, spread with herb butter, sandwich with thin slices of salmon fillet, then bake.

Pan-seared gravad lax on celeriac mash

225g/8oz celeriac
225g/8oz potatoes
salt and pepper
150ml/¼ pint milk
2 tbsp olive oil
1-2 tbsp sweet dill mustard

2 large dill pickles, chopped
8 spring onions, finely sliced
25g/1oz butter
450g/1lb sliced gravad lax

1 Peel the celeriac and potatoes and cut into even sized pieces. Add to a pan of cold salted water, bring to the boil and cook for 15-20 minutes until tender. Drain thoroughly, then mash well.
2 Heat the milk with the olive oil, mustard, dill pickles and spring onions. Beat into the celeriac and potato mash: keep warm.
3 Heat the butter in a heavy based frying pan until sizzling. Fry the gravad lax, in two batches, over a high heat until just starting to colour.
4 Pile the mash on to warmed serving plates and top with the gravad lax. Pour on any pan juices and serve immediately.

Thin slices of gravad lax are quickly fried in butter and served on celeriac and potato mash flavoured with dill pickles and spring onions.

Trout with dill cucumbers and capers

Serves 2
2 whole trout, cleaned
2 tbsp seasoned flour
25g/1oz unsalted butter
juice of ½ small lemon
½ dill cucumber, finely chopped

1-2 tsp capers
1-2 tbsp flat leaf parsley, roughly
   chopped
salt and pepper

1 Coat the trout in seasoned flour. Melt the butter in a large frying pan, then fry the trout for 5 minutes each side or until cooked and the skin is crisp. Lift on to warm plates.
2 Pour the lemon juice into the pan juices. Warm through with the cucumber, capers and parsley. Season to taste, then pour over the trout. Serve with a salad and potatoes.

Pan fried trout with a piquant sauce of lemon butter, capers, dill cucumber and parsley.

Spicy grilled sardines

4 garlic cloves, crushed
½ tsp hot paprika
1 tsp ground cumin
1 tbsp lemon juice
1 tbsp olive oil
salt and pepper
12-16 fresh sardines, depending
  on size, cleaned

For the salad
5 oranges
1 red onion, very thinly sliced
25g/1oz flat leaf parsley leaves,
  roughly torn
16 large black olives (optional)
extra virgin olive oil, for drizzling

1 Mix the garlic with the spices, lemon juice, olive oil and seasoning.
Rub this mixture all over the sardines to coat thoroughly. Set aside.
2 For the salad, peel and segment the oranges, discarding all white pith,
membrane and pips. Place the orange segments in a bowl with the red onion,
chopped parsley and black olives if using. Season with salt and pepper
to taste and drizzle with a little olive oil.
3 Preheat the grill. Place the sardines on the rack over the grill pan and
grill for approximately 2 minutes each side until cooked through. Serve
with the orange salad and warm crusty bread.

Note Before grilling the sardines, add a little water to the grill pan.
This will prevent any juices from the fish burning on the pan base, which
causes smoking.

Fresh sardines are grilled with a spicy garlic
coating and served with a refreshing
Moroccan orange salad.

Mussels steamed in a paper bag

Illustrated on previous pages

1.5kg/3lb 5oz fresh mussels in shells
2 tbsp olive oil
1 garlic clove, chopped
2 celery sticks, cut into fine julienne
  strips
1 red pepper, cored, seeded and
  finely sliced
1 red chilli, seeded and finely diced
1 tsp Szechuan peppercorns, crushed
4 tbsp teriyaki marinade

1 To clean the mussels if necessary, scrub in several changes of water, discarding any that do not close when sharply tapped. Pull off any 'beards' which are still attached.
2 Preheat oven to 230C/fan oven 210C/Gas 8. Heat the oil in a frying pan and add the garlic, celery, red pepper and chilli. Stir-fry over a brisk heat for 1 minute. Add the crushed peppercorns and take off the heat.
3 Cut four 30cm/12in squares of baking parchment. Divide the mussels between the paper squares, piling them in the centre. Top with the stir-fried vegetables and pour 15ml/1 tbsp teriyaki marinade over each portion. Bring the sides of the paper up over the mussels to enclose them like a bag; tie with cotton string. Place on a baking tray.
4 Place in the oven for 10 minutes or until the mussels open (squeeze bags to check). Serve immediately, in the paper bags!

Note Make sure guests discard any mussels which have not opened.

Mussels are quick and easy, especially if you buy ready cleaned ones and cook them in this unusual way.

Salt baked hake

Serves 2.
1 hake, about 600g/1lb 5oz, cleaned
1tbsp Maldon salt flakes
few fresh rosemary branches
lemon wedges, to serve

1 Preheat oven to 220C/fan oven 200C/Gas 7. Snip the fins off the fish, using kitchen scissors. Wash the fish under running cold water. Shake off excess moisture then, holding on to the tail, toss the fish in the salt so that it all adheres.
2 Lay the rosemary over the base of an ovenproof dish and place the fish on top. Immediately bake for about 20 minutes until cooked through.
3 To serve, carefully break away and discard the salted fish skin. Serve the fish accompanied by lemon wedges, warm bread and a tomato, olive and red onion salad.

Hake is an inexpensive white fish with a good flavour. Here it is baked in a salt crust to seal in the flavour and juices. The flesh stays moist and, surprisingly, it isn't too salty.

Plaice with anchovies and Parmesan

Illustrated on previous pages

8 plaice fillets, skinned
4 anchovy fillets, finely chopped
200ml/7fl oz double cream
5 tbsp fresh brown breadcrumbs
2 tbsp finely chopped parsley
8 tbsp finely grated fresh Parmesan
   cheese

1 Preheat oven to 220C/fan oven 200C/Gas 7. Halve each plaice fillet lengthways along the natural line. Dot with the anchovies.
2 Roll up each fillet from the thickest end. Arrange the fish, spiral side uppermost, in 4 individual gratin dishes and spoon over the cream.
3 Mix the breadcrumbs with the parsley and Parmesan and scatter over the plaice. Bake for 8-10 minutes until the fish is cooked and the topping is golden. Serve with a salad, or grilled tomatoes and baby potatoes.

Plaice fillets are rolled around chopped anchovies, then dotted with cream and baked under a cheese and herb crumb topping.

Cod with creamy white bean stew

2 tbsp olive oil
2 garlic cloves, finely chopped
2 tbsp finely shredded fresh sage
1 red chilli, seeded and finely
    chopped

400g can cannellini beans, drained
150ml/¼ pint fish or vegetable stock
50g/2oz butter
2 onions, halved and thinly sliced
4 cod steaks, each about 175g/6oz

1 Heat half the oil in a pan; fry the garlic until golden. Add the sage and chilli; cook for 1 minute. Add the beans and stock, bring to the boil and simmer for 20 minutes; season.
2 Meanwhile, melt the butter in a small pan. Stir in the onions, add 2 tbsp water and cover tightly. Simmer gently for 20-25 minutes until very soft, stirring occasionally.
3 Brush the cod steaks with oil, season and grill for 2-3 minutes on each side. Serve on the bean stew, topped with the onions.

Grilled cod steaks served on meltingly soft cannellini beans flavoured with chilli, garlic and sage, and topped with caramelised onions.

Steamed sea bass with fennel

Serves 2

1 tbsp olive oil

3 small fennel bulbs, trimmed and each cut into 8 wedges, feathery fronds reserved

½ tsp cardamom seeds (from 3-4 pods)

500ml/18fl oz vegetable stock

1 sea bass, about 750g/1lb 10oz, cleaned

salt and pepper

1 Heat the oil in a wide, heavy based deep pot or flameproof casserole, add the fennel with the cardamom seeds and fry until lightly browned and slightly softened.

2 Add the stock and bring to the boil. Lower the heat, cover and simmer for 10 minutes.

3 Season the fish and place on its side on top of the fennel. Cover tightly and cook over a medium heat for 15-20 minutes. To make sure the fish is cooked, insert a knife in the thickest part of the back and check that the flesh is opaque.

4 Carefully lift the fish on to a serving dish and surround with the fennel wedges. Spoon the pan juices over the fish and garnish with the reserved fennel fronds. Serve with warm crusty bread or plain boiled potatoes to mop up the juices.

Note Most white fish have low fat flesh because their oil is stored in the liver. Oily fish, such as sardines, salmon, tuna and trout, have oil distributed throughout their flesh and are therefore relatively high in fat but full of beneficial fish oils and vitamins.

The delicate flavours in this fragrant one-pot meal are retained during cooking.

easy
chicken

Chicken with pawpaw and rice noodles

Serves 2

225g/8oz skinless chicken breast
  fillets
100g/4oz rice vermicelli noodles
1 small carrot, cut into julienne or
  fine matchsticks
1 small pawpaw, peeled, seeded and
  diced
2 tbsp fresh coriander leaves,
  roughly torn

For the marinade

1 tbsp Thai fish sauce
1 tsp sesame oil
1 tsp Thai red curry paste
1 tsp clear honey

For the dressing

3 tbsp sunflower oil
1 tbsp caster sugar
3 tbsp lime juice
1½ tbsp Thai fish sauce or soy sauce
1 red chilli, seeded and chopped

1 First mix the marinade ingredients together in a dish. Cut the chicken into strips, toss in the marinade and leave for 1 hour.

2 Soak the noodles in boiling water for 4-5 minutes or according to pack instructions. Drain, dry well and place in a large bowl. Add the carrot, pawpaw and coriander.

3 Mix the dressing ingredients together, toss half with the noodles and chill until required.

4 Heat a wok or large frying pan until smoking. Add the chicken with the marinade and stir-fry over a high heat until cooked through. Divide the chicken and noodles between 4 bowls and serve drizzled with the remaining dressing.

This warm salad of hot, spicy chicken tossed with cool pawpaw, carrot and rice noodles epitomises the fresh tastes of Thai food.

Goujons with avocado mayonnaise

4 slices softgrain bread
2 tsp poppy seeds
¼ tsp cayenne pepper
2 tbsp snipped fresh chives
4 skinless chicken breast fillets,
   thickly sliced
2 eggs, beaten
4 tbsp sunflower oil, for frying

For the mayonnaise
1 large avocado, halved and stoned
3 tbsp mayonnaise
2 tbsp French dressing
salt and pepper

1 First blend the mayonnaise ingredients together in a food processor until creamy; turn into a bowl. Clean the processor.

2 Break the bread in to the food processor. Add the spices, chives and 1 tsp salt. Process to crumbs; tip on to a plate. Dip the chicken strips in the egg, then into the spicy crumbs to coat.

3 Heat the oil in a large non-stick frying pan and fry the goujons for 2-3 minutes each side until crisp and golden. Serve hot, with the avocado mayonnaise and a salad.

Poppy seeds, chives and cayenne add a savoury note to these crunchy chicken strips. An avocado dip is the perfect foil.

Seared chicken with marsala and sage

Serves 6

4 free-range chicken breast fillets,
  skinned
salt and pepper
2 tbsp sunflower oil

12 fresh sage leaves
85g/3oz butter
1 tbsp chopped fresh sage
175ml/6fl oz marsala

1 Cut each chicken fillet lengthways into 6 strips and season lightly. Heat the oil in a frying pan and fry the sage leaves a few at a time for a few seconds; lift out and drain on kitchen paper.

2 Melt some of the butter in a heavy-based pan and sear the chicken in batches over a high heat to brown all over. Return all chicken to the pan; add the chopped sage.

3 Pour in a little marsala. As it reduces to a syrup, continue to add marsala a little at a time until only about 2 tbsp remains. Lift the chicken onto warmed plates.

4 Deglaze the pan with the remaining marsala and pour over the chicken. Top with the fried sage leaves to serve.

This is quick enough to cook between courses. Serve on a large bread croûte with colourful salad leaves.

Rosemary and lemon chicken with olives

Serves 6

12 skinless boneless chicken thighs
1 unwaxed lemon, halved
6 tbsp olive oil
6 garlic cloves, peeled and halved
  lengthways
2 onions, halved and sliced

10 fresh rosemary sprigs
950g/2lb 2oz potatoes (preferably
  organic), peeled
1 tsp ground black pepper
2 tsp Malden salt flakes
18 kalamata olives

1 Trim the chicken thighs of any excess fat and cut them in half. Place in
a bowl, squeeze the lemon juice over the chicken and toss well; leave to stand
for 10 minutes. Discard one of the lemon shells; cut the other into slivers
and set aside.

2 Preheat oven to 220C/fan oven 200C/Gas 7. Drain the chicken and pat each
piece dry. Place in a large shallow roasting tin in a single layer. Mix in the
lemon slivers, olive oil, garlic, onions and 5 rosemary sprigs; leave to stand
for 20 minutes.

3 Cut the potatoes into 4cm/1½ inch pieces. Add to a pan of boiling water,
bring back to the boil and par-cook for 2 minutes only; drain well.

4 Add the potatoes to the chicken and sprinkle with the pepper and half of
the salt. Bake in the oven for 50 minutes, turning all the ingredients every
10 minutes. If there is a lot of liquid from the onions 10 minutes before the
end, increase the heat to 240C/fan oven 220C/Gas 9.

5 About 5 minutes before the end of the cooking time, replace the rosemary
with fresh sprigs, and add the olives. Serve sprinkled with the remaining
salt flakes.

As the flavours of this effortless all-in-one
meal are robust, serve simply with a well
dressed salad.

Lemon chicken with garlic and potatoes

Illustrated on previous pages

8-12 chicken pieces (thighs and
   drumsticks)
salt and pepper
finely grated rind of 1 lemon
2 tbsp chopped fresh thyme

900g/2lb small new potatoes
1 lemon, very thinly sliced
12 large garlic cloves (unpeeled)
150ml/¼ pint olive oil

1 Preheat oven to 180C/fan oven 160C/Gas 4. Put the chicken in a large
bowl, season well and add the lemon rind and thyme. Toss well to coat and
spread in a large baking dish.
2 Crack each potato by tapping sharply with a rolling pin. Add to the
chicken. Tuck the lemon slices around. Scatter the garlic cloves over
the chicken. Drizzle the olive oil evenly over the top.
3 Bake for about 45 minutes, stirring occasionally, until golden brown
and cooked through. Serve with courgettes or broccoli.

Try this as an alternative to the traditional
Sunday roast – it's all done in one dish!

Chicken with pancetta and asparagus

Serves 6

150g/51/2oz asparagus tips
6 free-range chicken breast fillets,
   skinned

salt and pepper
18 slices pancetta
2 tbsp olive oil
chervil or parsley sprigs, to garnish

1 Cook the asparagus in boiling water for 2 minutes, then drain and refresh in cold water; drain again and pat dry on kitchen paper.

2 Slice horizontally into each chicken breast without cutting all the way through, then open out. Place, two at a time, between sheets of greaseproof paper and beat with a rolling pin to flatten out slightly.

3 Preheat oven to 190C/fan oven 170C/Gas 5. Season each chicken breast lightly and cover with 1½ slices of pancetta. Place 4 asparagus tips lengthways on top and roll up. Brush the chicken parcels with a little oil and wrap each one in a further 1½ slices of pancetta.

4 Wrap each parcel tightly in foil to seal and hold in the juices. Place on a baking sheet and bake in the oven for 20 minutes.

5 Leave to rest in a warm place for 5-15 minutes, then remove the foil. Slice the chicken parcels into rounds and serve on a bed of rice, with any juices poured over. Garnish with chervil or parsley.

Note Packets of thinly sliced pancetta are available from larger supermarkets. Alternatively you can buy pancetta freshly sliced from Italian delicatessens.

These are very easy to prepare, hours in advance. Serve sliced to reveal the pretty asparagus and pancetta.

Chicken pies with butternut mash

500g/1lb 2oz butternut squash, peeled, seeded and diced
1 kg/2lb 4oz potatoes, peeled and diced
300ml/½ pint milk
1 tsp chopped fresh sage
25g/1oz butter
4 skinless chicken breast fillets, cut into 2.5cm/1in cubes
salt and pepper
1 small Bramley apple, peeled, cored and chopped
2 leeks, sliced
150ml/¼ pint dry cider
1 chicken stock cube
50g/2oz mature Cheddar cheese, grated

1 Put the butternut squash, potatoes, milk, chopped sage and butter in a pan and season with salt and pepper. Bring to the boil, lower the heat, cover the pan tightly and simmer for 20-25 minutes, stirring once, until the potatoes are tender. Mash until the mixture is smooth.

2 Meanwhile, put the chicken in a pan with the apple, leeks, cider and stock. Season, cover and simmer gently for 25 minutes until the leeks and chicken are tender and the apples are pulpy.

3 Spoon the chicken mixture over the base of four 350ml/12fl oz pie dishes and top with the mash. Sprinkle with the cheese. (If preparing ahead, cover and keep in the fridge until ready to cook.)

4 To serve, preheat oven to 190C/fan oven 170C/Gas 5. Bake the pies for 30 minutes until golden and piping hot. Serve with broccoli or cabbage.

Tasty pies filled with chicken, leeks and tart apple cooked in cider. Butternut squash gives a sweet, nutty flavour to the mash topping.

Skewered rosemary chicken

4 skinless chicken breast fillets, cut into 2.5cm/1in cubes
1 clove garlic, crushed
2 tsp chopped fresh thyme
juice of ½ lemon
salt and pepper
8 fresh rosemary stems, at least 23cm/9in long (preferably woody)

1 Put the chicken in a non-metallic bowl and add the garlic, thyme, lemon juice and seasoning. Toss well and leave to marinate for 30-40 minutes (no longer), turning occasionally.
2 Strip the rosemary stems of their leaves, except for the 7.5cm/3in at the narrow end. Cut the woody ends obliquely to shape points that will pierce the chicken.
3 Preheat the grill. Lift the chicken from the marinade, reserving the juice.
4 Thread the chicken pieces on to the skewers carefully and lay on the grill tray, with the leafy rosemary tips towards you.
5 Cover the rosemary leaves with a strip of foil to prevent them from scorching. Grill for about 10-15 minutes, turning and basting occasionally with the reserved marinade. Serve with a mixed salad.

Note Try using bay or sage branches instead of rosemary – the woodier the herb stems, the better. Or, for a quicker alternative, thread the chicken pieces onto pre-soaked wooden kebab skewers and sprinkle with a little chopped rosemary before grilling.

Grilling meat on herb skewers gives off a wonderful aroma to stimulate the tastebuds.

Lime and ginger grilled chicken

4 skinless chicken breast fillets
½ tsp finely grated lime rind
juice of ½ large lime
2.5 cm/1in piece fresh root ginger,
   finely shredded

salt and pepper
2 tsp maple syrup or clear honey
snipped chives, to garnish

1 Using a very sharp knife, score the chicken deeply in a criss-cross pattern, cutting halfway through the thickness. Place in a shallow dish.
2 Mix together the lime rind and juice, ginger and seasoning. Brush this over the scored surface of the chicken and leave to marinate for about 20 minutes.
3 Preheat the grill to high. Brush the chicken with the maple syrup or honey and cook for 7-8 minutes on each side, turning and basting at least twice.
4 Serve garnished with snipped chives and accompanied by steamed French beans or sugar snap peas.

Lean chicken breast fillets are deeply scored before marinating to encourage the flavours to permeate and ensure quick cooking.

Rancher's chicken

Serves 2
2 skinless chicken breast fillets
1 large tomato, finely chopped
2 tbsp hickory barbecue sauce
1 tbsp olive oil

4 rindless smoked streaky bacon
  rashers
50g/2oz mature Cheddar cheese,
  grated

1 Beat the chicken fillets with a rolling pin until flattened to an even thickness. Stir the tomato into the hickory sauce.
2 Heat the oil in a large cast-iron (or other grillproof) frying pan, add the chicken and bacon and fry for about 1-2 minutes each side. Preheat the grill.
3 Space the chicken fillets apart in the pan, then spread with the tomato mixture. Sprinkle with the cheese and top with the bacon.
4 Grill for about 3 minutes until the bacon is turning golden and the cheese has melted. Serve with a salad and jacket potatoes.

This takes minutes to make, yet the smoky sauce adds a special taste.

Chicken with lemon and minted couscous

Illustrated on previous pages

finely grated rind and juice of
  2 lemons
2 garlic cloves, crushed
2 tsp ground cumin
8-12 chicken pieces (thighs and
  drumsticks)
4 tbsp olive oil
salt and pepper

8 spring onions, sliced
350ml/12fl oz chicken stock
  (approximately)
6 tbsp chopped fresh mint
225g/8oz quick-cook couscous
lemon wedges and mint sprigs,
  to garnish

1 Preheat oven to 200C/fan oven 180C/Gas 6. Mix the juice and rind of 1 lemon with the garlic and cumin. Rub this mixture all over the chicken pieces.
2 Spoon 2 tbsp of the olive oil over the base of a baking dish and add the chicken. Season, then add 150ml/¼ pint water. Bake in the oven for 25-30 minutes.
3 Meanwhile, heat the remaining olive oil in a pan, add the spring onions and fry gently for 2-3 minutes until starting to colour. Stir in the remaining lemon rind and juice. Pour in the stock and bring to the boil.
4 Add the mint, then pour in the couscous in a steady stream, stirring briefly to mix. Cover, remove from the heat and leave to swell for 10 minutes. Fork through the grains to break up any lumps; re-cover and keep warm.
5 Transfer the couscous and chicken to warmed plates. If necessary, deglaze the baking dish with a little extra stock or water and drizzle the pan juices over the chicken and couscous. Serve garnished with lemon wedges and mint sprigs.

Simple baked chicken served on a bed
of lemon couscous flavoured with mint.

Tagliatelle with lime chicken

Serves 3-4

2 large skinless chicken breast
  fillets
2 tsp sesame oil
1 tbsp dark soy sauce
½ tsp chilli sauce
300g/10oz dried tagliatelle or
  linguine
4 spring onions, thickly sliced on
  the diagonal

For the sauce

300ml/½ pint chicken or vegetable
  stock (see note)
200ml carton coconut cream
1½ tsp Thai fish sauce
6 kaffir lime leaves, shredded
1 garlic clove, sliced
pinch of sugar
salt and pepper

For the garnish

coriander leaves

1 Cut the chicken into strips and toss with the sesame oil, soy sauce and chilli sauce. Cover and leave to marinate in a cool place for 1 hour.

2 Meanwhile, prepare the sauce. Place all the ingredients in a saucepan, bring to the boil and simmer until reduced by half. Pass through a fine sieve and keep warm.

3 Bring a large pan of salted water to the boil. Add the pasta and cook until al dente.

4 Meanwhile, heat a wok or large frying pan until hot. Add the chicken and stir-fry for 4-5 minutes until browned and cooked thorough. Add the spring onions, toss well and remove from the heat.

5 Drain the pasta and spoon into warmed bowls. Top with the chicken and spring onion mixture and drizzle over the lime sauce. Serve at once, garnished with coriander leaves.

Note For the sauce use homemade or bought fresh stock, available in cartons from supermarket chilled cabinets.

Chilli, sesame, chicken, noodles and a creamy lime sauce is a wonderful fusion of flavours.

Japanese chicken skewers

4 tbsp Japanese soy sauce
2 tbsp saké or medium dry sherry
1 tbsp caster sugar
8 boneless chicken thighs, skinned
For the cucumber salad
1 small cucumber
½ tsp salt

15g/½oz arame or hijiki seaweed
  (optional)
2.5cm/1in piece fresh root ginger,
  peeled
2 tbsp rice wine vinegar
1 tbsp caster sugar

1 Put the soy sauce, saké or sherry and sugar in a small pan and heat gently until the sugar is dissolved. Set aside to cool.
2 Cut the chicken into bite size cubes, place in a dish, add the soy mix and marinate for 2 hours. Soak 4 bamboo skewers in cold water for 20 minutes.
3 Thinly slice the cucumber lengthways, using a vegetable peeler. Sprinkle with the salt and leave to drain for 30 minutes. Rinse well, dry on kitchen paper and place in a bowl. (If using seaweed, pour on boiling water and soak for 10 minutes; drain, dry well and add to the cucumber.)
4 Using a garlic crusher, squeeze out as much juice from the ginger as possible and mix the ginger juice with the vinegar and sugar. Add to the cucumber, toss well and set aside until required.
5 Preheat the grill. Remove the chicken from the marinade and thread onto the bamboo skewers. Grill for 6-7 minutes, turning and basting with the marinade until the chicken is cooked through.
6 Serve the chicken skewers hot with the cucumber salad.

Note Saké, or Japanese rice wine, is available from oriental food stores and wine merchants. If unavailable, medium dry sherry may be substituted.

Japanese cooking uses few ingredients, flavours are light, and dishes are healthy and often quick to prepare.

Warm chicken and asparagus salad

300g/10oz medium asparagus,
  trimmed
4 chicken breast fillets, cut into
  strips
1 tbsp vegetable oil
salt and pepper
4 tbsp fresh mint leaves
100g/4oz baby spinach leaves

For the lemon grass dressing:
1 tbsp sesame oil
1 tbsp vegetable oil
1 tsp paprika
2 lemon grass stalks, thinly sliced
3 tbsp lime juice
1 tbsp honey
2 tbsp light soy sauce

1 Preheat the grill to medium. Blanch the asparagus in boiling water for
3 minutes; drain and pat dry.

2 Brush the chicken strips and asparagus with oil; and season with salt
and pepper. Place on the grill rack and grill for 3-4 minutes on each side,
or until the chicken is cooked through.

3 Meanwhile, make the dressing. Gently heat the oils in a small pan. Add
the paprika and lemon grass and cook for 1-2 minutes.

4 Arrange the mint and spinach leaves on plates and top with the asparagus
and chicken.

5 Add the lime juice, honey and soy sauce to the dressing and slowly bring
to a simmer. Pour the warm dressing over the salad to serve.

Note Char-grill the chicken strips and asparagus if you prefer.

An easy, elegant salad enhanced with a warm
oriental flavoured dressing.

Poussins stuffed with herb butter

Serves 6

6 spatchcocked poussins (see below)

For the herb butter

6 garlic cloves (unpeeled)

150g/5½oz unsalted butter, softened

3 tbsp finely chopped fresh tarragon

3 tbsp finely snipped fresh chives

salt and pepper

For the garnish

2 tbsp roughly torn flat leaf parsley

1 Simmer the garlic cloves in water to cover for 6 minutes until softened; drain and cool slightly. Snip the root end and squeeze out the garlic into a bowl. Crush and mix in the butter, tarragon, chives and seasoning.

2 Gently ease up the skin on the breast and upper part of the poussins' legs with your fingers to make a pocket for the herb butter, taking care to avoid puncturing the skin. Spread the butter over the flesh under the skin, then press down the loosened skin.

3 Thread 2 wooden skewers crosswise through each bird to hold it flat (from wing through to the opposite leg). Set aside until ready to cook.

4 Preheat the grill to medium and oven to 120C/fan oven 100C/Gas¼. Grill the poussins, in 2 batches if necessary, for 20-25 minutes turning occasionally until golden and cooked through. Keep warm in the oven. Scatter with parsley to serve.

Note Prepare the poussins to stage 3 up to a day in advance. Refrigerate, but bring to room temperature before cooking.

Serve these on a mound of buttered saffron couscous. In summer, barbecue rather than grill the poussins.

Citrus roast chicken

1 oven-ready chicken, about
  1.6kg/3½lb
olive oil, for brushing
2 tsp five peppercorn mixture,
  crushed

3 tbsp redcurrant jelly
juice of 1 pink grapefruit
pink grapefruit segments, to
  garnish

1 Preheat oven to 200C/fan oven 180C/Gas 6. Brush the chicken all over with olive oil, then sprinkle with the crushed pepper and salt. Place breast side down in a non-metal shallow ovenproof dish. Roast for 45 minutes.

2 Melt the redcurrant jelly in a pan over a low heat. Add the grapefruit juice and bring to the boil, stirring. Turn chicken breast side up and spoon over half of the glaze. Lower oven setting to 180C/fan oven 160C/Gas 4 and roast chicken for a further 45 minutes, or until cooked through, basting at intervals with more glaze.

3 Transfer the chicken to a serving dish, cover loosely with foil and rest in a warm place for 15 minutes. Skim off the oil from the pan juices and heat until bubbling.

4 Serve the chicken garnished with grapefruit segments, with the pan juices as a gravy.

Notes To calculate roasting time, allow about 20 minutes per 500g/1lb weight plus an extra 20 minutes at 200C/fan oven 180C/Gas 6.
To test that the chicken is thoroughly cooked, pierce the thickest part of the leg with a skewer and make sure that the juices run clear, not at all pink.

An original roast – flavoured with crushed mixed peppercorns and a fresh grapefruit and redcurrant glaze.

Sesame roast chicken

1 oven-ready chicken, about
   1.6kg/3½lb
3 tbsp sesame oil
3 tbsp soy sauce
2-3 tsp grated fresh root ginger
1 tsp sesame seeds

1 Preheat oven to 200C/fan oven 180C/Gas 6. Mix the sesame oil, soy sauce and ginger together and brush half inside and over the chicken.
2 Lay the chicken breast down in the roasting tin and roast for 45 minutes. Turn breast up and brush with more soy mixture. Roast for 20 minutes.
3 Brush over the last of the soy mixture, sprinkle with sesame seeds and roast for a further 25 minutes or until the chicken is cooked, reducing the setting to 180C/fan oven 160C/Gas 4 if the bird is browning too fast.

Note Roasting the chicken breast-side down to start with helps to keep the breast meat succulent and moist.

This oriental style roast is delicious served with ready-made plum sauce and a salad of shredded cucumber and spring onion.

Mango and chicken salad

4 cooked chicken breasts (preferably roasted)
2 large mangoes, peeled, halved and stoned
50g/2oz roasted cashew nuts
½ head of iceberg lettuce, shredded
For the dressing
120ml/4fl oz coconut milk
½ tsp ground coriander
1 tbsp Thai fish sauce
1 tbsp soft brown sugar
2 spring onions, finely sliced
1 tbsp finely chopped fresh mint
2 tsp finely chopped fresh lemon grass
salt and pepper

1 First make the dressing. Put the ingredients in a small pan and heat gently until the sugar is dissolved. Remove from the heat and set aside.
2 Cut the chicken and mango flesh into cubes or slices and place in a large bowl with the cashew nuts. Toss to mix.
3 Divide the shredded lettuce between plates and top with the chicken and mango mixture. Stir the dressing and pour over the salad to serve.

Variation Use paw paw (papayas) instead of mangoes.

Scented mango, roast chicken, cashew nuts and crisp lettuce in a Thai coconut dressing, flavoured with fresh mint and lemon grass.

Aromatic chicken parcels

8 large chicken drumsticks or
　thighs, skinned
sea salt and pepper
24 large fresh basil leaves, or 2 tbsp
　chopped fresh basil
a little oil, for brushing

1 Preheat oven to 200C/fan oven 180C/Gas 6.
2 Season the chicken generously with salt and pepper, then press 3 basil
leaves on to each drumstick or thigh, or roll each chicken piece in chopped
basil to coat.
3 Lightly oil the 4 baking parchment sheets in the centre only. Place
2 chicken pieces on the oiled part of each piece of paper. Fold up the two
short sides over the chicken and pleat them together at the top, then fold
over the two loose ends and pleat to make a fairly secure parcel.
4 Place the parcels on a baking tray and bake for about 30 minutes until
the chicken is cooked through. Serve with vegetables.

Note For the parcels you will need 4 sheets of baking parchment, each about
30x23cm/12x9in.

Cooking herb-coated chicken in parcels seals
in all of the flavour and moisture.

Pumpkin and chicken broth

1 tbsp oil
4 shallots, finely chopped
1 tsp grated fresh root ginger
2 lemon grass stalks, finely chopped
2 skinless chicken breast fillets

400g/14oz pumpkin flesh, cubed
1.2 litres/2 pints good quality
   chicken stock
4 tbsp chopped fresh basil
salt and pepper

1 Heat the oil in a large heavy-based pan and fry the shallots until soft.
Add the ginger and lemon grass; stir-fry for 1 minute.
2 Add the chicken and cubed pumpkin flesh. Cook, stirring, for 1 minute.
3 Pour in the stock. Bring to the boil, cover and simmer for 10-15 minutes
or until the chicken is cooked through and the pumpkin is tender.
4 Stir in the chopped basil and check the seasoning. Pour into warmed bowls
and serve.

Serve this fragrant Thai broth as a lunch or
light supper, with plenty of crusty bread.

Smoky chicken wings

12 large chicken wings
2 tbsp olive oil
juice of ½ lemon
2 tsp sweet chilli sauce
1 tsp Pimenton (smoked Spanish
 paprika) or sweet paprika

1 tbsp sun-dried tomato paste or
 tomato purée
1 garlic clove, crushed
salt and pepper
thyme sprigs, to garnish

1 Pre-soak 8 long wooden or bamboo skewers in cold water for 20 minutes. Mix the olive oil, lemon juice, chilli sauce, paprika, tomato paste and garlic together to form a thick sauce.

2 Preheat the grill (or barbecue). Cut off the very tips of the chicken wings. Thread 3 chicken wings onto 2 parallel skewers; repeat with the remaining wings and skewers.

3 Grill (or barbecue) for 15 minutes, turning twice, then brush liberally with the sauce. Grill (or barbecue) for a further 10-15 minutes until cooked through and nicely browned, turning and basting with the sauce from time to time.

4 Season and garnish with thyme to serve. Eat the chicken wings with your fingers!

Note The secret of these barbecued wings is to brush with the glaze towards the end of cooking rather than at the start, to avoid scorching them.

Grill or barbecue these spicy sweet-sour glazed chicken wings and serve with warm bread and a tomato salad.

Devilled chicken

2 tbsp olive oil
4 boneless chicken breasts (with
 skin)
2 garlic cloves, chopped
2 tbsp balsamic vinegar
6 tbsp dry white wine

4 tbsp well flavoured chicken stock
1 tbsp sun-dried tomato paste
½ tsp mild chilli powder
2 tbsp chopped fresh parsley
salt and pepper

1 Heat the olive oil in a frying pan, add the chicken, skin side down, and fry gently for 15 minutes, undisturbed.

2 Turn the chicken over, add the garlic and fry gently for a further 5-10 minutes until cooked through. Transfer to a warmed serving dish and leave to rest in a warm place while making the sauce.

3 Pour the balsamic vinegar, wine and stock into the pan, scraping up any sediment. Whisk in the tomato paste and chilli powder. Let bubble until reduced and syrupy. Stir in the parsley and any juices from the chicken; taste and season. Pour the devilled sauce over the chicken to serve.

A rich and fiery sauce made in minutes with the pan juices and dark balsamic vinegar.

Stir-fried chicken, pak choi and egg noodles

2 skinless chicken breast fillets
6 tbsp dark soy sauce
2 garlic cloves, crushed
1 tbsp cornflour
1 tbsp soft brown sugar
2 tsp grated fresh root ginger
250g pkt medium Chinese egg
  noodles

2 tbsp sunflower oil
2 carrots, cut into matchstick strips
4 tbsp dry sherry
8 spring onions, sliced diagonally
200g/7oz pak choi or bok choi,
  roughly shredded
175g/6oz bean sprouts
4 tbsp chopped fresh coriander

1 Cut the chicken into strips and mix with the soy sauce, garlic, cornflour, sugar and ginger. Cook the noodles according to the pack instructions.

2 Heat the oil in a wok and stir-fry the carrot until starting to soften. Add the chicken mixture and stir-fry for 2-3 minutes. Sprinkle in the sherry and allow to bubble until it is totally reduced.

3 Add the spring onions, pak choi and bean sprouts. Heat through, stirring, then add the drained egg noodles and chopped coriander. Toss well to mix and serve immediately, in warmed bowls.

This aromatic, colourful stir-fry is quick to assemble and cook. If pak choi is not available, use Chinese leaves instead.

Mexican enchiladas

2 tbsp olive oil
2 red peppers, seeded and thinly
  sliced
2 red onions, sliced
3 cloves garlic, crushed
2 red chillies, seeded and finely
  sliced
2 tsp ground coriander
2 tsp ground cumin

4 chicken breast fillets, cut into
  strips
salt and pepper
220g can refried beans
4 tbsp chopped fresh coriander
300ml/½ pint soured cream
8 flour tortillas
140g/5oz mature Cheddar cheese,
  grated

1 Heat the oil in a large pan, then add the peppers, onions, garlic and three quarters of the chilli. Stir-fry over a high heat for about 8 minutes until softened.
2 Stir in the ground spices, then add the chicken strips and seasoning. Cover and cook for 5 minutes.
3 Remove from the heat and stir in the refried beans, three quarters of the fresh coriander and 2 tbsp of the soured cream.
4 Lay the tortillas on a work surface. Divide the chicken mixture between them and roll up to enclose. Place in a large ovenproof dish and top with the remaining soured cream. Scatter over the cheese, remaining chilli and coriander. (If preparing ahead, cover and chill.)
5 When ready to serve, preheat oven to 190C/fan oven 170C/Gas 5. Cover the tortilla dish with foil and bake for 50 minutes. Remove the foil and bake for a further 10–15 minutes until golden and piping hot. Serve with an avocado and lettuce salad.

Spicy Mexican tortillas are filled with chicken, refried beans and coriander, then baked in soured cream with a cheese and chilli topping.

Chicken on a bed of bay leaves

2 tbsp olive oil
20 fresh bay leaves
4 skinless chicken breast fillets
salt and pepper

1 Heat the oil gently in a heavy-based pan or casserole. Cover the base of the pan with a layer of bay leaves, then lay the chicken breast fillets on top. Season, cover tightly and cook for 10-12 minutes.
2 Turn the chicken breasts over, re-cover and cook for a further 10 minutes or until cooked through. Serve the chicken with the pan juices and vegetables of your choice.

This unusual Italian way of cooking chicken imparts a unique flavour.

Chorizo and chicken gumbo

3 tbsp olive oil
2 tbsp plain flour
2 fresh bay leaves
1 large onion, finely chopped
4 celery sticks, thickly sliced
1 tbsp Cajun seasoning
1 tsp fresh thyme leaves
400g can peeled tomatoes in juice
700ml/1¼ pints chicken stock

2 large green peppers, seeded and
  cubed
140g/5oz okra, trimmed (halved if
  large)
8 skinless chicken thighs
200g/7oz piece chorizo sausage,
  skinned and diced
salt and pepper

1 Heat the oil in a large heavy-based pan or flameproof casserole. Stir
in the flour and bay leaves and cook gently for about 5 minutes, stirring
frequently until the flour is a nutty brown colour.
2 Tip in the onion and celery and cook gently for 5 minutes. Stir in the
Cajun seasoning and thyme leaves.
3 Pour in the tomatoes and stock, then stir in all the remaining ingredients,
seasoning with salt and pepper to taste. Cover and simmer for 40 minutes
until the chicken is tender. (If preparing ahead, cool and chill.)
4 When ready to serve, reheat on the hob until piping hot. Serve with mixed
basmati and wild rice or bread and a leafy salad.

Spicy Spanish chorizo gives this New Orleans
stew a rich flavour. Okra is an authentic
ingredient and its sticky juices help to thicken
the sauce.

Prawn and chicken laksa

1 tbsp vegetable oil
1 onion, finely chopped
2 tsp grated fresh root ginger
2 tsp crushed garlic
3 lemon grass stalks, finely chopped
1 tbsp ground coriander
2 tsp ground cumin
1 red chilli, seeded and thinly sliced
4 boneless chicken thighs, skinned
  and cut into bite size pieces

400ml/14fl oz coconut milk
200ml/7fl oz chicken stock
200g/7oz cooked peeled tiger prawns
6 tbsp finely chopped fresh
  coriander
salt and pepper
200g/7oz packet medium egg
  noodles

1 Heat the oil in a large heavy-based pan, add the onion, ginger, garlic and lemon grass, and cook gently until the onion is softened.
2 Add the spices and stir-fry for 1 minute, then add the chilli and chicken. Stir-fry for 2-3 minutes, then pour in the coconut milk and stock. Bring to a simmer and cook gently for 15-20 minutes. Stir in the prawns and coriander leaves; season.
3 Meanwhile cook the noodles according to the pack instructions; drain well. Divide between serving bowls and top with the prawn mixture to serve.

Fragrant lemon grass, spicy red chilli, fresh ginger and pungent coriander gives this Thai dish its distinctive character.

easy
meat

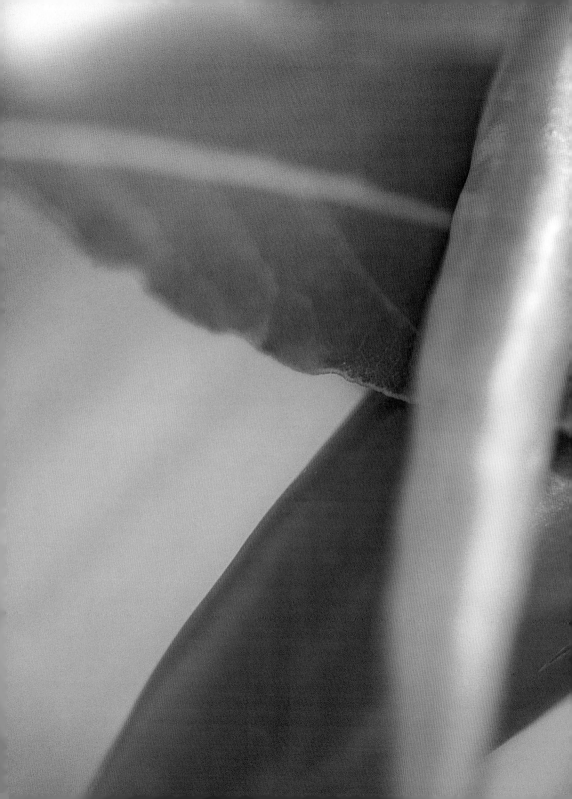

Honey, ginger and orange duck kebabs

6 duck breast fillets, each about
175g/6oz
grated rind and juice of 1 orange
4 tbsp clear honey
1 tbsp dark soy sauce
1 tsp ground ginger
1 tsp chilli powder

1 red pepper, halved, cored and
seeded
1 yellow pepper, halved, cored and
seeded
For the garnish
toasted sesame seeds
shredded spring onion

1 Remove the skin and fat from the duck breasts. Cut the meat into
4cm/1½in pieces and put into a shallow, non-metallic dish.
2 Mix together the orange rind and juice, honey, soy sauce, ginger and
chilli powder. Drizzle the mixture over the meat and turn to coat well.
3 Cut the peppers into 4cm/1½in squares and add to the meat. Toss well and
leave to marinate for 30 minutes.
4 Preheat the grill to high. Thread the duck and pepper pieces alternately
on to 8 metal skewers.
5 Place the kebabs on the grill rack and baste with the marinade. Grill for
about 10 minutes, turning and basting from time to time, until the peppers
are charred and the duck is evenly browned and cooked through.
6 Transfer the kebabs to warmed serving plates, allowing two per person.
Sprinkle over toasted sesame seeds and garnish with shredded spring onion.
Serve at once, accompanied by rice and a salad.

These tangy duck and sweet pepper kebabs
are best served with Thai jasmine rice and
a leafy salad.

Duck breasts with berry sauce

4 boneless duck breasts, each
   175-200g/6-7oz
salt and pepper
juice of 1 orange
4 tbsp redcurrant jelly with port

140g/5oz fresh or frozen mixed
   berries (red and blackcurrants,
   blackberries, raspberries and
   cherries)
½ tsp white wine vinegar

1 Preheat oven to 220C/fan oven 200C/Gas 7.

2 Score the duck breast fat and rub with salt. Preheat a large frying pan over a medium high heat. Add the duck breasts, skin side down, and cook for about 7 minutes until most of the fat is rendered from under the skin.

3 Turn the duck breasts over and seal briefly on the other side, then transfer to a rack over a roasting tin and roast for 15-20 minutes.

4 Meanwhile pour off the fat from the frying pan and wipe clean with kitchen paper. Add the orange juice, redcurrant jelly, berry fruits and wine vinegar to the pan. Season with salt and pepper to taste and let bubble until the sauce is syrupy.

5 Leave the duck to rest for a few minutes before carving into slices. Arrange on warmed serving plates and spoon over the berry sauce. Serve with sauté potatoes and green beans or mangetout.

Assorted berry fruits in an orange and redcurrant sauce cut the richness of duck to delicious effect.

Butterflied lamb with a spiced yoghurt crust

Serves 6-8

2kg/4½lb butterfied leg of lamb
1 tbsp dried green peppercorns,
    crushed
1 tbsp black peppercorns, crushed
3 garlic cloves, crushed
150ml/¼ pint Greek yogurt

1 Lay the meat, skin side down, and score the thicker parts as necessary
to make it an even thickness. Make slits all over the surface.
2 Mix the crushed peppercorns, garlic and yogurt together and rub this
mixture all over the cut surface of the lamb. Lay the meat in a shallow
dish, cover and then leave to marinate in the fridge for at least 1 hour,
preferably overnight.
3 Lift the lamb on to a foil-lined grill rack and cook under a medium hot
grill for 20 minutes each side, until medium.
4 Leave the meat to rest for 10 minutes before carving into long thin slices.
Serve with yogurt flavoured with chopped mint, and grilled naan bread.

Notes Ask your butcher to butterfly a leg of lamb for this recipe (ie. bone the
meat and open it out flat).
To barbecue, cook over medium hot coals for 15-20 minutes, then turn and
cook for a further 15-20 minutes.

Boneless flattened leg of lamb, rubbed with
crushed peppercorns, garlic and Greek yogurt
and grilled until meltingly tender.

Creole meatballs

600g/1lb 5oz lean minced lamb
1 onion, finely chopped
3 tbsp plain flour
1 tsp hot paprika
salt and pepper
oil for shallow-frying
For the creole sauce
1 tbsp vegetable oil
1 onion, finely chopped

2 red peppers, cored, seeded and
 chopped
3 garlic cloves, finely chopped
400g can chopped tomatoes
1 bay leaf
200g/8oz fresh pineapple, roughly
 cubed
200ml/7fl oz water

1 For the meatballs, put the minced lamb, onion, flour, paprika and
seasoning in a bowl and mix thoroughly. With wet hands, divide the mixture
equally into 16 pieces and shape into balls.

2 Heat the oil in a large frying pan and carefully fry the meatballs, turning
until evenly browned. Drain on crumpled kitchen paper and set aside.
Preheat oven to 200C/fan oven 180C/Gas 6.

3 To make the creole sauce, heat the oil in a frying pan and gently fry the
onion until softened. Add the red peppers and garlic; stir-fry for 1 minute.
Add the remaining ingredients, season well and bring to the boil, stirring.

4 Put the meatballs in a shallow ovenproof dish. Pour over the sauce and
bake in the oven for 20-25 minutes. Serve with plain boiled rice and a crisp
green salad.

Tender lamb meatballs cooked in a mildly
spiced creole sauce with fresh pineapple and
red peppers.

Lamb tagine

2 tbsp vegetable oil
1 large onion, finely chopped
2 garlic cloves, finely chopped
1kg/2¼lb boned shoulder of lamb,
  cut into 5cm/2in cubes
1 tsp saffron threads
1 tsp ground ginger

850ml/1½ pints lamb stock or water
250g/9oz ready-to-eat dried prunes
250g/9oz ready-to-eat dried apricots
2 tsp ground cinnamon
2 tbsp clear honey
salt and pepper

1 Heat the oil in a heavy based pan or flameproof casserole and sauté the onion and garlic until soft. Add the meat and fry, turning occasionally, until evenly browned.
2 Add the saffron, ginger and stock or water and stir well. Cover and simmer gently for 1½ hours or until the meat is tender, adding a little hot water if the stew appears to be a little too dry.
3 Add the prunes, apricots, cinnamon and honey. Season with salt and pepper to taste, re-cover and simmer for a further 15 minutes.
4 Taste and adjust the seasoning. Serve with steamed couscous or rice, and a salad or green vegetable.

A wonderful Moroccan stew of lamb and dried fruit, enriched with saffron, ginger, cinnamon and honey.

Lamb chops with sweet potatoes and garlic

Illustrated on previous pages

4 lean chump chops or 8 lamb
   cutlets
4 tbsp olive oil
1kg/2¼lb sweet potatoes, peeled and
   cubed
2 red onions, cut into wedges
8 garlic cloves (unpeeled)

1 tbsp light muscovado sugar
juice of 1 lemon
1 small lemon, halved and thinly
   sliced
1 tbsp fresh thyme leaves, plus
   8 sprigs
salt and pepper

1 Trim the lamb of any excess fat. Preheat oven to 220C/fan oven 200C/Gas 7.
2 Heat the olive oil in a large frying pan. Add the sweet potato cubes, onion
wedges, garlic and sugar and fry, stirring, over a high heat for about
5 minutes until the vegetables start to soften and caramelise. Transfer
to a roasting tin.
3 Add the lemon juice, lemon slices, thyme leaves and seasoning, then top
with the lamb chops and thyme sprigs.
4 Roast in the oven for 25-30 minutes until the lamb chops are cooked and
the sweet potatoes are tender. Serve garnished with thyme sprigs and
accompanied by spinach.

Sweet potatoes are sautéed with lemon, red
onions and fresh thyme, then topped with
lamb chops and quick roasted.

Rump steaks with wilted rocket

4 rump steaks, each 175g/6oz

For the marinade
5 tbsp red wine
2 garlic cloves, crushed
3 tbsp olive oil
salt and pepper

For the aioli
2 garlic cloves, peeled and crushed
1 egg yolk
3 tbsp walnut oil
100ml/3½fl oz light olive oil
lemon juice, to taste

To serve
100g/4oz rocket leaves

1 In a shallow dish, mix together the wine, garlic, olive oil and seasoning. Add the rump steaks and turn to coat well. Cover and leave to marinate for 30 minutes.

2 Meanwhile, make the aioli. Pound the garlic with 1 tsp salt in a small bowl. Stir in the egg yolk. Gradually whisk in the oils, a few drops at a time. Once half the oil is incorporated, add a squeeze of lemon juice. Whisk in remaining oil in a thin, steady stream. Taste and season or add lemon juice as required.

3 Remove steaks from marinade and pat dry on kitchen paper. Brush with a little olive oil. Preheat grill to medium. Put the steaks on the grill rack and cook for 3 minutes each side, or to taste.

4 Serve each steak topped with a pile of rocket leaves and accompanied by the aioli.

Note To barbecue, cook over medium hot coals for 2-3 minutes per side, or to taste.

Tender, marinated rump steaks served topped with rocket and accompanied by a delicious aioli – made with walnut oil.

Horseradish crusted roast beef

Serves 4-6
1.3kg/3lb boned, rolled rib of beef
salt and pepper
3 tbsp fresh breadcrumbs
2 tbsp hot horseradish sauce
2 tsp grated horseradish

1 Preheat oven to 200C/fan oven 180C/Gas 6. Pat the joint dry with kitchen paper if necessary. Season with salt and pepper.
2 Mix the remaining ingredients together to make a paste, then spread evenly all over the joint.
3 Put the meat into a roasting tin and roast in the oven for 45 minutes. Reduce oven setting to 180C/fan oven 160C/Gas 4 and roast for a further 45 minutes. Rest in a warm place for 10 minutes before carving. Serve with roast potatoes and vegetables of your choice.

Note Always bring a roasting joint to room temperature before cooking, as this will affect the timing.

The best partner for a beautifully cooked roast is a very sharp carving knife – it will make the meat go much further!

Beef with bacon, thyme and garlic

Serves 4-6

1.3kg/3lb boned, rolled sirloin or rib
  of beef

85g/3oz smoked bacon lardons

3 garlic cloves, cut lengthwise into
  wedges

15 small fresh thyme sprigs

salt and pepper

olive oil, for basting

1 Preheat oven to 200C/fan oven 180C/Gas 6. Cut about 15 slits in the beef
with a sharp knife and insert a piece of bacon, a wedge of garlic and a thyme
sprig into each one.

2 Season the joint all over with salt and pepper and rub with a little olive oil.

3 Roast in the oven for 1½-2 hours until cooked to your preference. Leave to
rest in a warm place for 10 minutes before carving. Serve with roasted new
potatoes and a selection of vegetables.

Note For a succulent roast, look for a joint with a good marbling of fat as
this will help to keep the meat moist during roasting.

Boned and rolled sirloin or rib of beef studded
with lardons, garlic slivers and thyme sprigs.

Corned beef hash cakes

4 tbsp sunflower oil
1 onion, halved and thinly sliced
1 red pepper, quartered, cored,
  seeded and thinly sliced
2 garlic cloves, sliced
550g/1¼ lb potatoes (unpeeled),
  coarsely grated

6 large eggs
2 tsp Worcestershire sauce
dash of Tabasco sauce
salt and pepper
4 spring onions, finely chopped
200g can corned beef, diced

1 Heat half of the oil in a large frying pan. Add the onion, red pepper, garlic and potatoes and fry, stirring, for 8 minutes until softened.
2 In a large bowl, beat 2 eggs with the Worcestershire sauce, Tabasco and seasoning. Add the potato mixture, spring onions and corned beef; mix together thoroughly. Divide into 4 portions and shape roughly into round cakes.
3 Heat the remaining oil in the frying pan. Add the potato cakes, cover and cook for 10 minutes. Turn the potato cakes over and cook for a further 5 minutes.
4 Meanwhile, poach the remaining 4 eggs in boiling salted water for 3 minutes or until cooked to your liking; lift out with a slotted spoon.
5 Serve the hash cakes topped with the poached eggs, and an extra few drops of Tabasco if liked.

Note If you do not have a frying pan large enough to hold all four hash cakes, use two pans rather then cook in batches.

This unusual, tasty supper also makes a great Sunday brunch. Serve a refreshing leafy salad to follow.

Bean casserole with chorizo

250g/9oz dried pinto beans
100g/4oz dried butter beans
1 tbsp olive oil
450g/1lb pickling or baby onions,
  peeled
225g/8oz thick smoked gammon
  steak, cubed
200g/7oz chorizo sausage, skinned
  and cut into chunks

1 each green and orange pepper,
  cored, seeded and cut into chunks
700g bottle or carton passata
425ml/¾ pint chicken stock
3 tbsp molasses
2 tbsp wholegrain mustard
4 fresh bay leaves
1 tbsp fresh thyme leaves
1 tsp paprika

1 Soak the pinto and butter beans separately in plenty of cold water overnight.
2 The next day, rinse the beans ad place in separate large pans. Add fresh
cold water to cover and bring to the boil. Fast boil the butter beans for
10 minutes; pinto beans for 20 minutes. Drain.
3 Heat the oil in a large pan. Add the whole onions and fry over a medium
heat for about 5 minutes, stirring frequently.
4 Add the gammon, chorizo and peppers and cook, stirring, for 3–4 minutes.
Pour in the passata and stock, then stir in the beans, molasses, mustard,
herbs and paprika. Cover and simmer gently, stirring often, for 45 minutes
or until the beans are tender. (If preparing ahead, cool, then chill.)
5 To serve, reheat in a pan over medium heat, if necessary, until piping hot.
Serve with garlic bread and a salad.

Molasses and spicy chorizo sausage gives this
rustic dish a wonderful depth of flavour.

Mexican beef stew with lime and chilli

3 tbsp vegetable oil
700g/1½ lb lean minced beef
1 large onion, finely chopped
1 green chilli, thinly sliced
4 tbsp lime juice
400g can chopped tomatoes
2 Granny Smith's apples, peeled, cored and roughly chopped

2 tbsp capers
salt and pepper
3 large potatoes, peeled and cut into 2cm/¾in cubes
1 garlic clove, finely chopped
2 tsp ground cumin
grated Cheddar cheese, to garnish

1 Heat 2 tbsp oil in a large heavy based frying pan. Add the beef and onion and fry, stirring, until the meat is browned.
2 Add the chilli, lime juice, tomatoes, apples and capers. Lower the heat, cover with a tight fitting lid and simmer for 25 minutes or until the meat is tender. Season to taste.
3 Par-boil the potatoes in salted water for 10 minutes; drain thoroughly.
4 Heat the remaining oil in a large, non-stick frying pan. Add the potatoes, garlic and cumin and fry, stirring, until golden brown.
5 Divide the spiced potatoes between warmed plates and top with the stew. Sprinkle with some grated cheese and serve with tortillas or crusty bread and a salad.

Known as picadillo in Mexico, this unusual stew is flavoured with fresh chilli, lime juice, apples and cumin. It is served on a bed of fried potatoes and topped with cheese.

Penne with venison and ceps

15g/½oz dried ceps, rinsed
150ml/¼ pint boiling water
2 tbsp olive oil
2 large onions, halved and sliced
700g/1½lb venison mince
150ml/¼ pint red wine
3 tbsp tomato paste
1 tbsp chopped fresh marjoram
salt and pepper

For the pasta and sauce
175g/6oz penne or other pasta
    shapes
50g/2oz butter
50g/2oz plain flour
600ml/1 pint milk
1 egg, beaten
175g/6oz mature Cheddar, grated
1 slice of bread, diced

1 Soak the dried ceps in the boiling water for about 15 minutes, then drain and chop, reserving the liquor.
2 Heat the oil in a large pan and gently fry the onions for 8-10 minutes, until golden. Add the venison and stir-fry until browned.
3 Pour in the wine and add the mushrooms with their soaking liquid. Stir in the tomato paste, marjoram and seasoning, cover and simmer for 10 minutes.
4 Cook the pasta in a large pan of boiling water until al dente; drain.
5 Meanwhile put the butter, flour and milk in a pan and whisk over a low heat until smooth and thickened. Stir in the pasta, season and let cool slightly, then beat in the egg and two thirds of the cheese.
6 Preheat oven to 190C/fan oven 170C/Gas 5. Spread the venison mixture in a large ovenproof dish. Spoon over the pasta and sauce, then top with the bread and the rest of the cheese. Bake the pasta in the oven for 40 minutes until bubbling and golden. Serve with a leafy salad.

Note Venison is a good low fat alternative to beef, although extra lean beef mince can be used here if preferred.

Minced venison in a rich stock flavoured with dried mushrooms and fresh marjoram, baked under a cheesy pasta topping.

Venison steaks with juniper and ginger

4 venison steaks, each 175g/6oz
olive oil, for brushing
salt and pepper

For the butter
175g/6oz unsalted butter
1 tbsp finely chopped fresh root
    ginger
3 juniper berries, finely chopped
1 tsp coarse sea salt

1 For the flavoured butter, beat the butter in a bowl until very soft, then beat
in the ginger, juniper berries and salt. Shape into a log, wrap and chill for
1 hour until firm.
2 Preheat grill to medium. Brush the venison steaks with olive oil and
season well. Place on the grill rack and grill for 3-4 minutes on each side.
3 Serve the venison steaks topped with slices of the flavoured butter.

Grilled lean venison steaks topped with slices
of savoury butter flavoured with fresh ginger,
sea salt and juniper berries.

Spiced pork escalopes with apricots

Illustrated on previous pages

Serves 2-3

450g/1lb pork fillet (tenderloin), cut into 1cm/½in slices
1 tsp powdered cloves
salt and pepper

6 fresh apricots, stoned and quartered
3 whole cloves
6 tbsp water
2 tsp clear honey

1 Lay the pork slices between sheets of greaseproof paper and beat with a rolling pin to flatten. Sprinkle with the ground cloves, salt and pepper.
2 Heat a large non-stick frying pan until very hot. Cook the pork in batches for about 1 minute each side until tender; transfer to a warmed dish, cover and keep warm in a low oven while cooking the sauce.
3 Add the apricots and whole cloves to the pan and cook, shaking the pan, for 2-3 minutes until they are lightly singed. Add the water and honey, scraping up the sediment. Continue to cook until the apricots are softened but still hold their shape, adding a little more water if needed.
4 Serve the meat topped with the apricots and pan juices. Accompany with French beans or steamed courgettes.

Variations Use fresh plums or crisp apple wedges instead of apricots.

Tender pork fillet, beaten thin, cooks quickly without losing its juiciness. Fresh apricots spiced with cloves are the perfect foil.

French-style bacon steaks

1½ tbsp sunflower oil
4 thick mild cure bacon steak
  rashers
2 small red apples, cored and cut
  into wedges

2 tbsp Calvados or brandy
1 tsp green peppercorns in brine,
  crushed
2 tsp Dijon mustard
200ml carton crème fraîche

1 Heat the oil in a large frying pan and fry the bacon steaks for about
3 minutes, turning once. Lift from the pan; set aside.
2 Add the apples to the pan and sauté for 1 minute or until beginning to
colour. Add the Calvados, then stir in the peppercorns, mustard and crème
fraîche to make a creamy sauce.
3 Return the bacon steaks to the pan to heat through before serving. Serve
with mashed potatoes and stir-fried cabbage.

A chunky apple sauce spiked with Calvados,
Dijon mustard and green peppercorns cuts the
richness of smoked bacon steaks.

Spiced crisp belly pork

Serves 4-6

1.25kg-1.3kg/2¾-3lb piece belly
  pork, boned
salt
1 tsp Thai seven spice mix
300g/10oz shallots, finely sliced
6 garlic cloves, finely chopped

2 fat red chillies, seeded and finely
  chopped
2 tbsp sunflower oil
4 tbsp clear honey
100ml/3½fl oz white wine
3 tbsp dark soy sauce
coriander sprigs, to garnish

1 Using a very sharp knife, deeply score the pork skin through to the fat
at 1cm/½in intervals. Rub in plenty of salt and leave to draw out moisture
for 1-1½ hours.

2 Preheat oven to 200C/fan oven 180C/Gas 6. Dry the pork skin well with
kitchen paper and rub in the spice mix. Place in a shallow roasting tin and
roast for 25 minutes. Mix the shallots, garlic and chillies with the oil.

3 Spoon the shallot mixture under the pork and roast for 50 minutes
or until the skin is very crisp.

4 Brush with 2 tbsp honey and return to the oven for 10 minutes. Brush
with another 1 tbsp honey; roast for a final 10 minutes.

5 Transfer the pork and shallots to a serving plate and rest in a warm place
until the sauce is ready. Pour off the fat from the tin, place on the hob and
add the wine, soy and remaining honey, stirring to deglaze.

6 Cut the meat into squares. Serve on a bed of rice, with the sauce and
shallots. Garnish with coriander sprigs.

This is perfect with steamed bok choi and
sticky Thai rice. Buy organic belly pork if you
can – its thick skin is easier to score.

Pork and prosciutto madeira meatballs

Illustrated on previous pages

350g/12oz pork mince
70g/2½oz prosciutto
1 large garlic clove, crushed
25g/1oz white bread
salt and pepper
1 medium egg

2 tbsp sunflower oil
4 tbsp Madeira
125ml/4fl oz pork or chicken stock
6 sage leaves, shredded
150ml/¼ pint double cream
450g/1lb dried linguine or spaghetti

1 Put the pork mince and prosciutto in a food processor and pulse briefly to chop the ham. Add the garlic, bread, ½ tsp salt, a generous grinding of pepper and the egg. Process until well mixed.
2 Divide the mixture into 4 pieces, then shape 6 meatballs from each portion.
3 Heat the oil in a large frying pan and fry the meatballs, turning, until golden. Add the madeira and bubble until reduced by half.
4 Pour in the stock, stir in the sage and season. Simmer gently for 5 minutes, then stir in the cream.
5 Meanwhile, add the linguine to a large pan of boiling salted water and cook until al dente. Drain and toss with the meatballs and sauce. Serve with steamed Savoy cabbage.

These meatballs are surprisingly quick to make and taste superb.

Glazed bacon and mango pockets

4 boneless bacon chops, each
   175g/6oz
olive oil, for brushing
salt and pepper
For the glaze
2 tbsp fine cut orange marmalade
finely grated rind and juice of 1 lime

For the salsa
1 large mango, halved, peeled and
   stoned
finely grated rind and juice of 1 lime
1 small red chilli, seeded and
   chopped
2 tbsp chopped fresh coriander

1 For the glaze, warm the marmalade together with the lime rind and juice
until melted.
2 Cut 4 thin slices from the mango; chop the rest. Mix the chopped mango
with the remaining salsa ingredients and set aside.
3 Make a horizontal slit in the side of each bacon chop and slip in a slice
of mango; secure with a cocktail stick. Brush with olive oil and season well.
4 Preheat grill to medium. Put the bacon chops on the grill rack and grill
for 5 minutes each side, brushing with glaze for the last minute on each
side. Serve with the mango salsa.

Bacon chops are stuffed with a slice of mango,
flavoured with a tangy citrus glaze, then
served with a mango salsa spiked with chilli.

Hickory'n'maple ribs

8 meaty pork ribs, about 1.3kg/
  3lb in total
For the marinade
125ml/4fl oz maple syrup

3 tbsp hickory barbecue sauce
juice of 1 small lemon
1 tbsp sweet chilli sauce
2 garlic cloves, crushed

1 Put the pork ribs in a shallow non-metallic dish. Mix all the marinade ingredients together in a bowl, then pour the mixture over the ribs and turn to coat well. Cover and leave to marinate in the fridge for up to 2 days.
2 Preheat oven to 190C/fan oven 170C/Gas 5. Transfer the ribs to a large, shallow roasting tin and baste with the marinade. Cover the tin loosely with foil and bake for 40 minutes, then uncover and bake for a further 40 minutes, basting occasionally, until the meat is tender.
3 Serve the pork ribs accompanied by jacket potatoes and coleslaw or warm bread and a leafy green salad.

Variation Replace the marinade with a hot, spicy sauce. Mix together 6 tbsp tomato ketchup, 4 tbsp Worcestershire sauce, 2 tbsp Dijon mustard, 4 tbsp muscovado sugar and a dash of Tabasco sauce. Marinate the ribs in the mixture and cook as above. Serve with garlic bread and a salad.

Smoky hickory sauce and maple syrup
enhance meaty spare ribs to delicious effect.

easy
vegetables
and
salads

Sabzi pulao

400g/14oz basmati rice
2 tbsp vegetable oil
1 onion, halved and thinly sliced
6 cardamom pods
6 cloves
1 cinnamon stick
225g/8oz mushrooms, roughly
  chopped

2 carrots, cut into cubes
1 red pepper, cored, seeded and
  roughly chopped
225g/8oz frozen peas
1 tsp saffron threads, soaked in
  2 tsp hot water
salt and pepper
crisp fried onion slices, to garnish

1 Rinse the rice in a large sieve under cold running water until the water
is clear; drain thoroughly.
2 Heat the oil in a large heavy based pan and sauté the onion over a medium
heat until lightly browned.
3 Add the cardamom pods, cloves and cinnamon. Stir-fry for 1 minute, then
add the rice and fry, stirring, for a further 1 minute. Add the vegetables and
stir well.
4 Stir in 750ml/1½ pints boiling water, the infused saffron and seasoning.
Cover tightly. Simmer on a very low heat for 15 minutes.
5 Leave to stand, covered, for 10 minutes then fluff up the rice with a fork.
Serve garnished with crisp fried onions.

Serve this one pot meal with hot pickles,
yogurt, and a cucumber and tomato salsa.

Vegetable pie with Parmesan crust

For the vegetable filling
300ml/½ pint vegetable stock
1 fennel bulb, halved and sliced
3 leeks, sliced
3 carrots, sliced
3 courgettes, thickly sliced
3 tbsp pesto
salt and pepper

For the Parmesan topping
175g/6oz self-raising flour
85g/3oz butter, in pieces
50g/2oz fresh breadcrumbs
100g/4oz Parmesan, freshly grated
4 tbsp buttermilk (or half
    yogurt/half milk)

1 Preheat oven to 200C/fan oven 180C/Gas 6. Bring the stock to the boil in
a pan. Add the fennel, leeks and carrots, cover and simmer for 10 minutes.
Stir in the courgettes, pesto and seasoning to taste; cook for 5 minutes.
2 For the topping, tip the flour into a food processor, add the butter with
a little seasoning and process until incorporated.
3 Add the breadcrumbs and Parmesan to the processor and pulse until
evenly mixed, then add the buttermilk (or yogurt and milk) and process
briefly until the mixture forms small clumps.
4 Spoon the vegetables into a 2.3 litre/4 pint ovenproof dish and cover with
the topping. Bake for 20-25 minutes until the topping is firm and golden.
Serve with a leafy salad.

Pesto enriched vegetables topped with
a cheesy crumbly pie crust.

Stuffed beefsteak tomatoes

Illustrated on previous pages

Serves 2

4 large beefsteak or marmande
  tomatoes
85g/3oz dried pastina (small soup
  pasta)
salt and pepper
1 tbsp olive oil

1 red onion, diced
1 garlic clove, crushed
2 tsp finely chopped fresh oregano
100g/4oz mushrooms, diced
25g/1oz Parmesan or pecorino
  cheese, finely grated

1 Preheat oven to 180C/fan oven 160C/Gas 4. Cut off the tops of the
tomatoes; set aside for 'lids'. Using a teaspoon, scoop out the tomato seeds
and cores to leave 1cm/½in thick shells.

2 Add the pasta to a pan of boiling salted water and cook until al dente.
Drain and rinse in cold water to arrest cooking; drain thoroughly.

3 Heat the olive oil in a pan, add the onion and cook gently for 5 minutes
until softened but not coloured. Add the garlic and cook for 2-3 minutes.
Add the oregano and mushrooms and fry gently for a further 3-5 minutes.
Allow to cool slightly. Add the grated cheese, pasta and seasoning to taste;
mix well.

4 Spoon the mushroom filling into the hollowed-out tomatoes, then replace
the tomato lids. Carefully transfer to an ovenproof dish and bake for about
30 minutes until the tomatoes are quite soft but still holding their shape.
Serve hot.

Juicy giant baked tomatoes filled with small
pasta, mushrooms, Parmesan and oregano
make a tempting vegetarian meal.

Radicchio, asparagus and black beans

500g/1lb 2oz thin asparagus,
  trimmed to 13cm/5in lengths
2 radicchio, each cut into 6 wedges
4 garlic cloves, crushed
½ tsp dried chilli flakes
8 tbsp extra virgin olive oil

salt and pepper
200g/7oz cooked black beans (see
  note), or canned black, aduki or
  red kidney beans
4 tsp balsamic vinegar

1 Put the asparagus and radicchio in a large shallow dish. Add the garlic, chilli flakes, 4 tbsp oil and seasoning. Turn the vegetables to coat well.
2 Preheat a ridged griddle pan or heavy based frying pan over a medium heat, then cook the asparagus for 2 minutes on each side. Return to the dish.
3 Add the radicchio to the pan and cook for 1 minute each side; add to the asparagus.
4 Put the black beans in a pan with some of their liquid. Warm through, then drain and add to the vegetables. Toss to mix and check the seasoning.
5 Serve warm or cold, drizzled with the balsamic vinegar and remaining oil.

Note To obtain this weight of cooked beans, soak 100g/4oz dried black beans in cold water overnight. Drain, put into a pan and cover with fresh water. Bring to the boil and boil fast for 10 minutes, then lower the heat and simmer for 1½ hours or until tender.

This wonderful combination of flavours is perfect for a vegetarian meal. Serve warm or cold, with char-grilled flat bread if you like.

Bubble and squeak cake

Illustrated on previous pages

Serves 3-4

1kg/2¼lb potatoes, peeled and cubed
450g/1lb green cabbage, cored and
    shredded
2 leeks, thinly sliced
1 tsp salt
1 tsp coarsely ground black pepper

50g/2oz butter
200ml/7fl oz milk
140g/5oz chorizo sausage, skinned
    and chopped (optional)
2 tbsp sunflower oil
chopped parsley, to garnish

1 Add the potatoes to a large pan of boiling salted water, bring to the boil and position a steamer on top. Put the cabbage and leeks in the steamer and cook for 20 minutes.

2 Drain the potatoes and mash with the seasoning, butter and milk until smooth and creamy. Stir in the cabbage, leeks and chorizo sausage if using. Allow to cool. (If preparing ahead, cover and chill.)

3 To cook, heat 1 tbsp oil in a large heavy based frying pan. Add the potato mixture and press down evenly to make a cake. Fry over a medium heat for 10 minutes.

4 Turn the cake out on to a large plate. Heat the remaining oil in the frying pan, then slide the potato cake back into the pan and fry the other side for 5--10 minutes until golden and heated through. Serve at once, scattered with plenty of chopped parsley and accompanied by grilled tomatoes.

Spanish chorizo adds a unique flavour to this traditional dish, but it can be omitted for vegetarians.

Cracked wheat pilaf, chestnuts and fennel

4 red onions, peeled with root end intact
4 small fennel bulbs, trimmed with root end intact
6 tbsp olive oil
salt and pepper

250g/9oz cracked (bulgar) wheat
700ml/1¼ pints well flavoured vegetable stock (preferably homemade)
200g/7oz cooked peeled chestnuts
3 tbsp chopped flat leaf parsley

1 Preheat oven to 220C/fan oven 200C/Gas 7. Cut each onion and fennel bulb lengthways into 6-8 pieces. Place on a baking tray and drizzle with half of the oil. Season with salt and pepper and turn well to coat the vegetables with the oil.
2 Rinse the cracked wheat and drain well. Heat 2 tbsp oil in a heavy based flameproof casserole. Add the cracked wheat and stir to coat with the oil. Pour in the stock and bring to the boil. Lower the heat, cover and simmer gently for 15-20 minutes.
3 Meanwhile, roast the vegetables in the oven for 20 minutes.
4 When the cracked wheat is ready, turn off the heat, remove the lid and cover with a clean tea towel or muslin.
5 Add the chestnuts to the vegetables, turn to coat with oil and return to the oven for a further 5 minutes. Fold the vegetables into the cracked wheat with the remaining 1 tbsp oil and the chopped parsley to serve.

Variation Serve the pilaf cold, with a herb vinaigrette folded through.

A simple, flexible vegetarian meal. Try using a mixture of herbs, add canned aduki beans or scatter with toasted pine nuts.

Vietnamese salad

Illustrated on previous pages

4 tbsp lime juice

3 tbsp caster sugar

salt and pepper

1 red onion, halved and finely sliced

250g/9oz white or Savoy cabbage,
very finely shredded

1 large carrot, roughly grated

2 cooked boneless chicken breasts,
skinned

2 tbsp vegetable oil

3 tbsp fresh mint leaves, roughly
torn

2 tbsp fresh coriander leaves,
roughly torn

1 tbsp roasted peanuts, roughly
chopped

1 Mix the lime juice, sugar, ½ tsp salt and ½ tsp pepper in a bowl. Add the onion and leave to marinate for 30 minutes.

2 In a large, shallow serving bowl, toss the cabbage and carrot together.

3 Cut the chicken into strips, and add to the salad with the onion, marinade and oil. Toss well to mix.

4 Just before serving, fold in the chopped mint and coriander and then scatter over the roasted peanuts.

Light, crisp cabbage salad, also known
as Vietnamese coleslaw.

Spiced okra and potato stew

500g/1lb 2oz potatoes, peeled
2 tbsp vegetable oil
1 onion, halved and thinly sliced
2 garlic cloves, finely chopped
2.5cm/1in piece fresh root ginger, finely chopped
1 red chilli, halved and finely sliced
2 tsp cumin seeds
½ tsp turmeric

2 tsp ground coriander
300ml/½ pint vegetable stock or water
400g can chopped tomatoes
450g/1lb small okra, tips trimmed (see note)
salt and pepper
3 tbsp chopped fresh coriander leaves

1 Cut the potato into 2.5cm/1in cubes. Heat the oil in a large pan, add the onion and cook gently for 10-15 minutes until soft and golden. Add the garlic, ginger, chilli and spices; fry, stirring, for 1 minute. Add the potatoes and mix well.

2 Pour in the stock and bring to the boil. Lower the heat, cover and simmer for 5 minutes.

3 Stir in the tomatoes and cook briskly for 5 minutes, then add the okra. Season well with salt and pepper, cover and simmer gently for 15 minutes, stirring occasionally. Off the heat, stir in the chopped coriander. Serve with warm naan bread.

Note To trim okra, remove a small piece from each end. Do not cut right into the pods or you will release the sticky juices inside and the stew will acquire an unpleasant glutinous texture during cooking.

A delicious, spicy stew flavoured with ginger, cumin, chilli and coriander.

Warm mushroom, ham and sweet potato salad

Serves 2

25g/1oz butter

1 small sweet potato, peeled and
  diced

100g/4oz small chestnut
  mushrooms, halved

80g pkt Black Forest ham, each slice
  halved

50g/2oz baby spinach leaves

25g/1oz watercress sprigs

For the dressing

3 tbsp extra virgin olive oil

1 tbsp tarragon or red wine vinegar

1 garlic clove, crushed

1 tsp chopped fresh tarragon

1 tbsp chopped fresh basil

salt and pepper

To garnish

basil sprigs

1 Melt the butter in a frying pan, add the sweet potato and fry, stirring frequently, for 8-10 minutes until tender and golden.

2 Meanwhile, mix the dressing ingredients together in a bowl, seasoning with salt and pepper to taste.

3 Remove sweet potato from the pan; keep warm. Add the mushrooms to the pan and fry for 3-4 minutes until softened. Add the ham and cook for 1-2 minutes.

4 Put the spinach and watercress on to serving plates. Scatter with the mushrooms, ham and sweet potato croûtons. Drizzle with the dressing and serve garnished with basil.

Note If Black Forest ham is unobtainable, use Parma ham instead.

A substantial warm salad, topped with sweet potato croûtons.

Frisée, pancetta and aubergine salad

Illustrated on previous pages

100g/4oz sliced smoked pancetta, derinded
4 tbsp olive oil
4 slices white bread, about 100g/4oz, crusts removed, cut into cubes
2 garlic cloves, crushed
vegetable oil, for deep-frying

1 aubergine, thinly sliced
100g/4oz frisée leaves
For the dressing
6 tbsp extra virgin olive oil
1½ tbsp balsamic vinegar
salt and pepper

1 Grill the pancetta for 2-3 minutes each side until crisp and golden. Cool, then crumble into bite size pieces.
2 Heat the olive oil in a frying pan. Fry the bread cubes for a few minutes until golden all over, adding the garlic for the last minute. Drain on some kitchen paper.
3 Heat a 5cm/2in depth of oil in a heavy pan to 160C. Deep-fry the aubergine slices in batches for 1-2 minutes until crisp. Drain on kitchen paper; keep warm in the oven.
4 Put the frisée in a large bowl and add the bacon and croûtons. Whisk the dressing ingredients together, then pour over the salad and toss lightly. Serve in individual bowls, topped with the aubergine crisps.

Note Smoked pancetta is available from Italian delicatessens and selected supermarkets. If unobtainable, use lightly smoked bacon instead.

Crisp fried aubergine slices add a new dimension to this classic salad.

Couscous salad with apricots and almonds

225g/8oz couscous
large pinch of saffron threads
300ml/½ pint hot vegetable stock
75g/3oz ready-to-eat dried apricots,
    chopped
75g/3oz raisins
3 tbsp chopped fresh mint

3 tbsp chopped fresh flat leaf parsley
finely grated zest of 1 lemon
3 tbsp extra virgin olive oil
salt and pepper
squeeze of lemon juice, to taste
2 tbsp flaked almonds, toasted

1 Put the couscous into a bowl, add the saffron threads, then pour on the hot stock and leave to absorb for 10 minutes.

2 Add the apricots and raisins to the warm couscous, fork through and set aside until cool.

3 When cold, add the chopped mint and parsley, grated lemon zest and olive oil. Season with salt and pepper to taste and toss to mix. Finish with a generous squeeze of lemon juice. Scatter with the toasted almonds to serve.

Variation For a more lemony flavour, add 40g/1 1/2oz chopped preserved lemon with the herbs.

This fruity couscous salad can be prepared in advance and kept in the fridge, but bring it back to room temperature to serve.

Shredded cabbage with fruit and pistachios

Illustrated on previous pages

Serves 4-6

600g/1lb 5oz white cabbage, cored
and finely shredded
1 yellow grapefruit
1 pink grapefruit
1 orange
100g/4oz raisins (preferably large
semi-dried raisins)

1 small bunch fresh chives, snipped
1 tbsp walnut oil
salt and pepper
50g/2oz shelled roasted salted
pistachio nuts, roughly chopped
(100g/4oz weight in shells)

1 Place the shredded cabbage in a large bowl.
2 Cut away all the skin and white pith from the grapefruit and orange then, with a sharp knife, carefully cut the flesh from between the membranes. Do this over the bowl of cabbage, to catch the fruit and citrus juices.
3 Add the raisins, chives, oil and seasoning; toss gently together.
4 Just before serving, toss in the chopped pistachio nuts.

A wonderfully refreshing, juicy side salad –
colourful enough to tempt even the most
jaded of palates.

Courgette, cucumber and rocket salad

4 medium courgettes
175g/6oz piece cucumber, diced
100g/4oz rocket leaves
salt and pepper
extra virgin olive oil, for drizzling

1 Coarsely grate the courgettes, using a hand grater or a food processor fitted with a coarse grating disc. Turn into a bowl.
2 Add the cucumber to the courgette and toss to mix. Add the rocket leaves and toss carefully. Season with salt and pepper.
3 Arrange the salad in a shallow bowl and drizzle with olive oil to serve.

Simply dressed with olive oil, so as not to disguise the delicate flavours, this fresh tasting salad is great with chicken or fish.

Chicory, radish and red onion salad

Illustrated on previous pages

4 heads of chicory, cut into chunks
1 bunch red salad radishes,
   quartered
1 red onion, very finely sliced

For the dressing
1 bunch watercress, stalks removed
4 tbsp extra virgin olive oil
1 tbsp white wine vinegar
1 tsp black peppercorns
salt

1 Put the salad ingredients in a bowl of iced water while making the dressing.
2 Whizz the watercress leaves, oil, vinegar and black peppercorns in a blender or food processor until almost smooth. Taste and season with salt – it should be quite peppery.
3 Drain and dry vegetables. Toss with half of the dressing and then place in a salad bowl. Drizzle with remaining dressing to serve.

A crunchy side salad with a vivid green, peppery dressing of puréed watercress.

New potato salad with chervil and chives

675g/1½lb Jersey Royals or other
  new potatoes, scrubbed
salt and pepper
4 tbsp mayonnaise
2 tbsp Greek yogurt

1 tsp wholegrain mustard
2 tbsp chopped fresh chervil or flat
  leaf parsley
2 tbsp chopped fresh chives
squeeze of lemon juice

1 Add the new potatoes to a pan of cold salted water, bring to the boil and simmer for 12–15 minutes until just tender.
2 Meanwhile, combine the mayonnaise and yogurt in a large bowl and stir in the mustard. Season with salt and pepper to taste.
3 Drain the potatoes in a colander and cool slightly, then toss with the dressing and chopped herbs while still warm. Add a squeeze of lemon juice and check the seasoning. Serve warm or at room temperature.

Chervil is a delicately flavoured herb that goes well with potatoes; if unobtainable, simply use flat leaf parsley instead.

Baby beets with orange and walnuts

16 baby beetroot with leaves
(2 bunches)
4 oranges
4 tbsp olive oil
salt and pepper
85g/3oz walnut halves

1 Preheat oven to 190C/fan oven 170C/Gas 5. Cut the tops from the beetroot; set aside. Scrub the beetroot and put in a baking dish.
2 Finely grate the rind from 2 oranges and squeeze the juice. Add this rind and juice to the beetroot with half the olive oil, and seasoning; toss to coat. Cover with foil and bake for 45 minutes or until tender.
3 Meanwhile, peel and segment the remaining oranges, discarding all of the membrane and pips.
4 Heat the remaining oil in a frying pan and add the beetroot tops. Sauté for 2-3 minutes until wilted and tender. Stir in the orange segments and walnuts. Season generously with salt and pepper.
5 Add the baked beetroot to the wilted beet tops. Toss to mix well and then serve immediately.

Young beetroot – bought in bunches – are best baked to retain all their earthy flavour. Combined with orange, walnuts and their leafy tops, they make a great accompaniment.

Spiced roast potatoes with garlic

1.1kg/2½lb potatoes, peeled and cut
  into 5cm/2in chunks
2 tbsp plain flour
1 tbsp smoked paprika or mustard
  powder

1 tsp salt
4 tbsp vegetable oil
2 garlic bulbs, cloves separated
  (unpeeled)

1 Preheat oven to 220C/fan oven 200C/Gas 7. Put the potatoes in a large pan and add cold water to cover. Bring to the boil and boil steadily for 5 minutes. Immediately drain and leave, uncovered, to cool slightly.
2 Mix together the flour, paprika or mustard and salt. Put the oil in a roasting tin and heat in the oven for a minute or two.
3 Meanwhile, toss the potato chunks in the spice mix to coat well. Carefully add to the hot oil, with the garlic cloves. Roast in the oven for 40-50 minutes until the potatoes are crunchy and browned, turning halfway through cooking. Serve piping hot.

Potato cubes, tossed in smoked paprika or mustard powder and roasted in olive oil with whole garlic cloves for a tasty accompaniment.

Mashed potatoes with horseradish

900g/2lb floury potatoes, peeled and
    cut into chunks
salt and pepper
200ml/7fl oz soured cream
2 tbsp grated hot horseradish
1 tbsp olive oil or butter

1 Add the potatoes to a large pan of cold salted water, bring to the boil and boil for 15-20 minutes until very tender.
2 Drain well, then shake the potatoes in the covered pan to drive off moisture. Let rest in the pan with the lid ajar for a few minutes.
3 Meanwhile warm the cream, horseradish and oil or butter together in a small pan.
4 Mash the potatoes with the horseradish cream until smooth. Season and serve.

This tasty mash is delicious served topped with fried breadcrumbs spiked with extra grated horseradish.

Roasted squash with shallots

2 butternut squash, each about
   450g/1lb
50g/2oz butter
3 tbsp maple syrup

12 shallots, peeled
12 garlic cloves (unpeeled)
2 tbsp raisins
salt and pepper

1 Preheat oven to 200C/fan oven 180C/Gas 6. Halve the squash, scoop out the seeds, then peel. Cut the flesh into large chunks.

2 Melt the butter with the maple syrup in a roasting dish. Add the shallots and squash, toss to coat and bake for 20 minutes.

3 Add the garlic cloves and raisins and bake for a further 20 minutes or until the squash and garlic are tender and beginning to caramelise. Season generously and serve.

Sweet butternut squash enriched with caramelised shallots and earthy roast garlic. Serve with roast pork, turkey or duck.

Roasted tomatoes and pepper salad

Illustrated on previous pages

2 red peppers, halved, cored and
   seeded
2 yellow peppers, halved, cored and
   seeded
6 tbsp olive oil

6 ripe plum tomatoes, quartered and
   cored
12 large garlic cloves (unpeeled)
2 tbsp balsamic vinegar
salt and pepper

1 Preheat oven to 200C/fan oven 180C/Gas 6. Cut each pepper half into
3 or 4 thick strips. Toss with the olive oil and place in a baking tin. Bake
for 15 minutes.
2 Stir in the tomatoes and unpeeled garlic cloves and roast for a further
15-20 minutes or until the garlic cloves are soft and the peppers begin
to colour.
3 Lift out the roasted vegetables and garlic with a slotted spoon and place
in a warm serving dish. Swirl the balsamic vinegar into the pan juices.
Bring to the boil and let bubble for 30 seconds, then pour over the tomatoes
and peppers.
4 Season with salt and pepper to taste and serve immediately or allow to cool
to room temperature; do not refrigerate.

A gutsy, colourful cooked salad inspired by
the flavours of the Mediterranean. Serve as an
accompaniment to grilled meat or poultry.

Hassleback potatoes

8 even sized, slightly oval potatoes,
  each about 140g/5oz
2 tbsp truffle oil, or extra virgin
  olive oil
1 small bunch (or packet) fresh
  thyme
sea salt

1 Preheat oven to 220C/fan oven 200C/Gas 7. Slice each potato vertically
across its width at 3mm/⅛in intervals, without cutting right through. Rinse,
then put the potatoes in a bowl of chilled water for 15 minutes; they will
open out slightly. Drain and dry well.
2 Brush the oil between the potato slices and all over the skin. Push a small
thyme sprig into each slit. Season with salt.
3 Place each potato on a 20cm/8in square of foil, pull up the corners and
twist loosely. Put the parcels on a baking sheet and bake in the oven for
40 minutes. Fold back the foil slightly and bake for a further 30-40 minutes
until the potatoes are cooked.

These thyme scented, fanned roast potatoes
are excellent with poultry and game.

Bok choi with shiitake mushrooms

600g/1lb 5oz bok choi or pak choi,
  stems removed
2 tbsp vegetable oil
3 large garlic cloves, finely sliced
6 spring onions, finely sliced
350g/12oz shiitake mushrooms,
  thickly sliced

½ tsp coarsely ground black pepper
1½ tbsp caster sugar
1 tsp sesame oil
1 tbsp rice wine or rice wine vinegar
3 tbsp dark soy sauce
To serve
sesame oil, for drizzling (optional)

1 Separate and roughly chop the bok choi leaves. Add to a large pan of boiling water and cook for 2 minutes; drain thoroughly and set aside.
2 Heat the oil in a large wok. Add the garlic, spring onions, mushrooms and pepper, and stir-fry for 4-5 minutes.
3 Add the sugar, sesame oil, rice wine and soy sauce. Stir-fry for 2 minutes, then add the blanched bok choi, toss well and heat through.
4 Serve at once in warmed bowls, drizzled with a little sesame oil if wished and accompanied by rice or noodles.

Quick and easy Chinese stir-fried vegetables, flavoured with soy, sesame and rice wine.

Potato and celeriac rösti

700g/1½lb floury potatoes (King
  Edward or Romano)
salt and pepper
350g/12oz celeriac, peeled

1-2 tsp fennel seeds (optional)
2 tbsp olive oil
50g/2oz butter

1 Put the unpeeled potatoes in a large pan of cold salted water with the celeriac. Bring to the boil and par-cook for about 8-10 minutes. Drain and leave until cool enough to handle, then peel the potatoes.
2 Coarsely grate the potatoes and celeriac into a large bowl and toss in the fennel seeds if using; mix well. Season with salt and pepper to taste.
3 Heat 1 tbsp of the oil in a 23cm/9in sauté pan and add half of the butter. When melted and foaming, tip in the potato mixture and spread evenly; don't press down too firmly. Cook over a moderate heat for about 15 minutes, shaking the pan from time to time to prevent the rösti from sticking.
4 Invert a plate over the pan, then turn the rösti out on to the plate. Add the remaining oil and butter to the pan and heat until foaming. Slide the rösti back into the pan and fry the uncooked side for 15-20 minutes, shaking the pan occasionally. Serve cut into wedges.

An excellent accompaniment to poultry and game, especially chicken and duck breasts.

Courgette, chilli and sugar snap sauté

3 tbsp olive oil
4 medium courgettes, cut into broad strips
175g/6oz sugar snap peas or mangetout
1 plump green chilli, halved, seeded and finely chopped
2 tbsp soured cream
3 tbsp chopped fresh coriander
salt and pepper

1 Heat the olive oil in a frying pan or sauté pan and add the courgettes and sugar snaps. Stir-fry for 3 minutes, then add the chilli and stir for 1 minute. Remove from the heat.
2 Stir in the soured cream and coriander. Season and serve at once.

A fast stir-fry of green vegetables with a hint of chilli, enriched with a little soured cream.

Peas with cherry tomatoes and spinach

Illustrated on previous pages

225g/8oz shelled fresh or frozen peas
150ml/¼ pint dry white wine
2 tbsp olive oil
1-2 fresh bay leaves

175g/6oz whole ripe cherry tomatoes
225g/8oz fresh leaf spinach, stalks
  removed (see note)
salt and pepper

1 Place the peas in a large pan with the wine, olive oil and bay leaves. Bring to the boil, then lower the heat and simmer gently for 5 minutes.
2 Add the cherry tomatoes and simmer for a further 5 minutes until tender and the liquid is well reduced.
3 Finally, stir in the spinach and cook for a few minutes, turning occasionally, until the leaves just wilt.
4 Season with salt and pepper to taste. Serve immediately.

Note For convenience, buy bags of ready prepared spinach from supermarkets. Otherwise, choose small, tender spinach leaves and wash thoroughly in several changes of water to remove all traces of grit. Drain thoroughly before cooking.

This is a sort of quick vegetable stew – very colourful and full of goodness! Serve with grilled or roast meat or poultry.

Moroccan spiced cauliflower with mint

Serves 4-6
1 medium cauliflower, divided into
  florets
85g/3oz butter
1 tsp sweet paprika

½ tsp ground cumin
½ tsp ground coriander
salt and pepper
handful of fresh mint leaves

1 Steam the cauliflower over boiling water for 10-12 minutes until just tender. Remove and allow to dry a little.
2 Melt the butter in a frying pan. When sizzling, add the spices and fry, stirring, for 30 seconds. Add the cauliflower florets and stir to coat with the buttery spices. Season well with salt and pepper.
3 Add the mint leaves and cook gently until wilted. Serve immediately.

Cauliflower is lightly steamed until tender, then tossed in a Moroccan spiced melted butter with fresh mint leaves.

easy
desserts
and bakes

White chocolate and berry creams

500g bag frozen mixed summer fruits (raspberries, blackberries, redcurrants etc.)

3 tbsp icing sugar

4 tsp cassis, framboise or kirsch

200g/7oz white chocolate, in pieces

150g carton whole milk raspberry yogurt

500g carton fromage frais with added cream

white chocolate curls or grated chocolate, to decorate

1 Tip the frozen fruits into a bowl, stir in the icing sugar, then spoon into 4 wide stemmed glasses and drizzle over the liqueur.

2 Put the chocolate in a large heatproof bowl over a pan of simmering water until just melted. Remove from the heat, then beat in the yogurt and fromage frais until smooth.

3 Spoon the chocolate mixture over the fruit and leave in a cool place to allow the fruits to defrost slowly.

4 Serve topped with chocolate curls or grated chocolate.

Tart summer berries under a contrasting blanket of smooth, creamy white chocolate are an irresistible combination.

Amaretto and blueberry syllabubs

For the blueberry layer
2 x 170g punnets blueberries
1 tbsp amaretto liqueur
1 tbsp caster sugar
For the syllabub
284ml carton double cream
2 tbsp caster sugar

90ml/3fl oz medium white wine,
 such as Riesling
3 tbsp amaretto liqueur
8 amaretti biscuits, broken into
 small pieces
To decorate
mint leaves

1 Tip the blueberries into a large pan. Add the liqueur and sugar and poach gently for 1-2 minutes until the berries have softened, but have not burst. Allow to cool.
2 To make the syllabub, pour the cream into a bowl. Add the sugar, wine and liqueur, and whisk until the mixture holds its shape.
3 Toss the blueberries with the amaretti biscuits, then layer with the creamy syllabub in 4 stemmed glasses. Chill until required.
4 Serve the chilled syllabubs decorated with mint leaves.

Note Fresh gooseberries, apricots and plums all make excellent alternatives to blueberries. Stone and quarter plums or apricots. Adjust the sugar accordingly and poach until the fruit is tender, but still retaining shape.

Topped with an almond flavoured syllabub, poached blueberries make an elegant, quick dessert – ideal for mid-week entertaining.

Pan-fried banana with orange and cardamom

50g/2oz unsalted butter
50g/2oz light muscovado sugar
5 cardamom pods, lightly crushed
4 bananas, peeled and halved
    lengthways
grated rind and juice of 1 large
    orange

1 Melt the butter in a large frying pan, then add the sugar with the
cardamom and stir until the sugar is dissolved.
2 Add the bananas and cook for 1-2 minutes, turning them in the juices,
until softened. Add the orange juice and rind and let bubble until reduced
and syrupy. Discard the cardamom pods.
3 Serve hot, with vanilla ice cream.

Cardamom adds an exotic flavour to this
hot dessert. Vanilla ice cream is the perfect
accompaniment.

Caramelised apples on brioche toasts

3 tbsp caster sugar
3 Cox's apples, peeled, cored and
   thickly sliced
25g/1oz butter
large pinch of ground cinnamon

3 tbsp raisins
juice of 1 lemon
4 thick slices of brioche (from a
   large cottage brioche)
250g carton Greek yogurt

1 Sprinkle the sugar over the base of a large frying pan and heat gently
until it melts and begins to caramelise – don't allow to darken.
2 Add the apples and toss to coat, then add the butter, cinnamon, raisins,
lemon juice and 1 tbsp water. Cook, turning frequently, for 1-2 minutes.
3 Meanwhile, toast the brioche slices under a hot grill until golden on both
sides. Place on serving plates.
4 Spoon the yogurt on to the brioche and top with the caramelised apples
and pan juices to serve.

Butter enriched brioche makes a delicious
base for pan-fried apple slices.

Plum and hazelnut crumble cake

8-10 slices
225g/8oz self-raising flour
1½ tsp baking powder
1 tsp ground cinnamon
140g/5oz unsalted butter, softened
140g/5oz caster sugar
3 large eggs, beaten
115g/4oz ground hazelnuts
6-8 plums, halved and stoned

For the crumble topping
25g/1oz plain flour
25g/1oz rolled oats
25g/1oz chilled butter, finely diced
50g/2oz light muscovado sugar
50g/2oz hazelnuts, roughly chopped

1 Preheat oven to 180C/fan oven 160C/Gas 4. Grease and base line a 25x20cm/10x8in baking tin. Sift the flour with the baking powder and ground cinnamon.
2 Cream the butter and sugar together in a bowl until pale and fluffy, then gradually beat in the eggs, adding a little of the flour with the last of the egg, to prevent curdling.
3 Fold in the remaining flour mixture and ground nuts. Spoon into the prepared tin and level the surface.
4 Arrange the plums cut side up over the cake, pressing down gently. Mix the crumble ingredients together and scatter over the top.
5 Bake for 45-50 minutes until risen, lightly golden, and a skewer inserted into the centre comes out hot. Leave in the tin for 10 minutes, then remove. Serve warm, with custard or crème fraîche.

Variation Use ground almonds instead of hazelnuts, and apricots in place of plums.

A warm cinnamon scented hazelnut sponge, covered with fresh plum halves and topped with a rich nutty crumble.

Glazed mille feuilles

8 small sheets filo pastry (each about 21x19cm/12½x7½in)
50g/2oz butter, melted
8 tbsp icing sugar, sifted
115g/4oz mascarpone
4 tsp rosewater essence

150ml/¼ pint double cream
400g/14oz mixed soft fruit, such as raspberries, strawberries, redcurrants, blueberries and blackcurrants
mint leaves, to decorate (optional)

1 Preheat oven to 200C/fan oven 180C/Gas 6. Lay a sheet of filo on a clean surface (keep the rest covered). Brush with melted butter, then layer 3 more sheets on top, brushing all except the top sheet with butter. Repeat to make another stack with the remaining filo.

2 Cut each stack into 6 triangles, it won't matter if they are a little uneven. Place on baking sheets and dust with approximately 2 tbsp of the icing sugar. Bake for 10-12 minutes until crisp and golden.

3 Pop under a hot grill (not too close to the element) for 15-30 seconds to glaze. Transfer to a wire rack to cool.

4 For the filling, beat the mascarpone with 4 tbsp icing sugar and the rosewater until smooth. Lightly whip the cream in another bowl, then gently fold into the mascarpone.

5 To assemble, layer 3 filo triangles per serving with mascarpone cream and fruit. Top with a sprig of redcurrants, and mint leaves if using. Just before serving, dust with the remaining icing sugar.

Note For convenience, prepare ahead to the end of stage 4. Assemble the mille feuilles 2 hours before serving.

These impressive filo stacks – layered with mascarpone and berries – are deceptively easy.

Melon, mint and ginger salad

Serves 8
1 medium Galia melon
1 Charantais or Cantaloupe melon
¼ small watermelon

2.5cm/1in piece fresh root ginger,
  peeled and roughly chopped
1 tbsp freshly torn mint leaves
mint sprigs, to decorate

1 Halve the whole melons. Scoop out the seeds from all 3 melons, then cut the flesh into chunks and place in a large bowl, adding any juices.
2 Put the ginger in a clean garlic press, hold over the melon bowl and press firmly, to extract the ginger juice. Add the mint leaves and toss gently. Chill until required.
3 Just before serving, toss the salad lightly and scatter with mint sprigs.

A refreshing, healthy fruit salad with the zing of freshly pressed ginger. Melons at their peak of ripeness are essential.

Peaches in elderflower champagne

Serves 6-8
6-8 peaches, ripe but firm
100ml/3½fl oz elderflower cordial
375ml/13fl oz (½ bottle) dry
   Champagne or good quality
   sparkling white wine

1 Preheat oven to 200C/fan oven 180C/Gas 6. Arrange the peaches closely in a deep ovenproof dish (just large enough to hold them in a single layer).
2 Measure the elderflower cordial into a jug, add the Champagne or sparkling wine, then pour the mixture over the peaches. Cover the dish with a lid, or with greaseproof paper then a layer of foil to seal.
3 Bake for 40-50 minutes or until the peaches are tender right through. If they are not fully submerged in the liquid, turn them over halfway through the cooking time.
4 Leave the peaches to cool in the syrup. If preferred, lift out and peel off the skins, then return the peaches to the elderflower Champagne to serve.

Luxuriously steeped in Champagne sweetened with a little elderflower cordial, these peaches make a mouthwatering summer dessert.

Raspberry yogurt ice

Serves 4-6
500g/1lb 2oz raspberries
2 tbsp light muscovado sugar
6 tbsp maple syrup
500ml/18fl oz organic yogurt

1 Put the raspberries and sugar in a blender or food processor and work to a purée, then pass through a sieve into a bowl to remove the seeds.
2 Stir the maple syrup and yogurt into the raspberry purée.
3 Freeze in an ice cream maker if you have one, according to the manufacturer's instructions. Alternatively, pour the fruit mixture into a freezerproof container and place in the coldest part of the freezer until partially frozen. As the ice crystals begin to form around the edges, remove the container from the freezer and whisk the raspberry mixture to break up the ice crystals. Return to the freezer. Repeat this process once more, then freeze until firm.
4 If necessary, transfer the yogurt ice to the fridge 30 minutes before serving to soften.

This wonderfully fresh-tasting ice relies on the use of flavourful, ripe raspberries.

Strawberry yogurt ice

Serves 4-6
150g/5oz caster sugar
175ml/6fl oz water
500g/1lb 2oz strawberries
500ml/18fl oz organic yogurt

1 Dissolve the caster sugar in the water in a small pan over a low heat. Increase the heat, bring to the boil and boil steadily until the syrup registers 107C on a sugar thermometer. Allow to cool.

2 Put the strawberries in a blender or food processor and work to a purée, then pass through a sieve into a bowl to remove the seeds. Stir in the sugar syrup, followed by the yogurt.

3 Freeze in an ice cream maker if you have one, according to the manufacturer's instructions. Alternatively, pour the fruit mixture into a freezerproof container and place in the coldest part of the freezer until partially frozen. As the ice crystals begin to form around the edges, remove the container from the freezer and whisk the strawberry mixture to break up the ice crystals. Return to the freezer. Repeat this process once more, then freeze until firm.

4 If necessary, transfer the strawberry yogurt ice to the fridge approximately 30 minutes before serving to soften.

Make this refreshing ice during the summer, when fragrant, homegrown strawberries are available.

Lime and papaya posset

Serves 6
600ml/1 pint double cream
175g/6oz caster sugar
finely grated rind of 1 lime
juice of 2 limes
2 papayas, peeled, seeded and
    chopped

1 Put the cream and sugar in a pan, heat gently until the sugar is dissolved, then boil for 3 minutes. Add half of the lime rind and all of the lime juice; stir well. Leave to cool for about 10 minutes.
2 Set aside 6 pieces of papaya; divide the rest between 6 individual glass bowls, then pour the lime mixture on top. Top with the lime rind and reserved papaya. Chill until ready to serve.

Note Perfectly ripe papayas are essential for this dessert.

Papaya has a special affinity with lime and the combination works beautifully in this dessert.

Triple chocolate brownies

Illustrated on previous pages

Makes about 12

115g/4oz butter, plus extra for greasing

85g/3oz good quality plain dark chocolate (minimum 70% cocoa solids), in pieces

4 medium eggs, beaten

2 tsp vanilla extract

400g/14oz caster sugar

115g/4oz plain flour

25g/1oz cocoa powder

115g packet milk chocolate drops

115g packet white chocolate drops

8 butterscotch sweets, roughly chopped

1 Preheat oven to 190C/fan oven 170C/Gas 5. Butter a 28x18cm/11x7in shallow baking tin and line the base with non-stick baking parchment.

2 Melt the butter with the chocolate in a heatproof bowl over a pan of simmering water. Remove from the heat and stir in the beaten eggs, vanilla extract and sugar. Mix thoroughly.

3 Sift the flour with the cocoa powder over the mixture, then beat in until evenly incorporated. Stir in the chocolate chips and butterscotch pieces.

4 Spoon the mixture into the tin and spread evenly. Bake in the middle of the oven for about 35 minutes until set on the surface, but still moist in the middle. Leave to cool in the tin.

5 Turn out when completely cold and cut into squares or bars to serve.

Note These chocolate brownies have a characteristic fudge-like texture. For a more 'cakey' texture, bake for an extra 5-10 minutes.

Irresistible rich, fudgey chocolate brownies, laden with milk and white chocolate chips, and butterscotch pieces.

Orange almond cake with rosewater cream

8-10 slices
6 large eggs, separated
175g/6oz caster sugar
grated rind of 2 oranges
juice of 1 orange
225g/8oz ground almonds

For the rosewater cream
2 cardamom pods, seeds extracted
2 tbsp rosewater essence
1 tbsp caster sugar
300ml/½ pint double cream

1 Preheat oven to 180C/fan oven 160C/Gas 4. Grease and base line a 23cm/ 9in spring release cake tin.
2 In a bowl, whisk the egg yolks, sugar and orange rind together until pale and thick. Stir in the orange juice, then fold in the ground almonds.
3 In a clean bowl, whisk the egg whites until just peaking, then fold into the cake mixture.
4 Spoon the mixture into the prepared tin and bake for 45-50 minutes until risen and firm to touch, covering loosely with foil after 20 minutes, if the cake appears to be overbrowning.
5 Meanwhile, for the cream, lightly crush the cardamom seeds and put in a small pan with the rosewater and sugar. Warm gently to dissolve the sugar. Allow to cool, then strain.
6 Whip the cream in a bowl, slowly adding the cooled syrup, until it forms soft peaks.
7 Serve the cake cut into wedges, accompanied by the rosewater cream.

A lovely light almond sponge with a hint of orange, accompanied by an exotic rosewater and cardamom cream.

Lemon polenta cake

8-10 slices

115g/4oz polenta (ordinary or quick-cook), plus extra for dusting
115g/4oz plain flour
1½ tsp baking powder
2 large eggs, plus 3 egg whites
175g/6oz caster sugar
grated rind of 2 lemons

125ml/4fl oz lemon juice (juice of 2-3 lemons)
1 vanilla pod, seeds extracted
100ml/3½fl oz vegetable oil
150ml/¼ pint buttermilk

To serve (optional)
crème fraîche
strawberries

1 Preheat oven to 180C/fan oven 160C/Gas 4. Grease and base line a 25cm/10in spring release cake tin. Dust the tin out with a little polenta.
2 Sift the flour and the baking powder together into a bowl, then stir in the polenta.
3 In a separate bowl, whisk the whole eggs, egg whites and sugar together until pale and thick.
4 Add the polenta mixture, lemon rind and juice, vanilla seeds, oil and buttermilk. Carefully fold into the whisked mixture, using a large metal spoon.
5 Spoon the mixture into the prepared tin and bake for 30 minutes, or until a skewer inserted into the centre comes out clean. Transfer to a wire rack and leave to cool completely.
6 Cut into slices and serve with crème fraîche and strawberries if you like.

Polenta colours this cake a pretty shade of yellow and adds a subtle crunch. Strawberries and crème fraîche are the perfect complement.

Focaccia with figs and raisins

Serves 4-6

115g/4oz seedless raisins
150ml/¼ pint medium or sweet
  sherry
225ml/8fl oz hand-hot water

2 tsp active dried yeast
2 x 145g packets instant pizza mix
85g/3oz demerara sugar
6-8 fresh figs, sliced
olive oil, for drizzling

1 Oil a 28x18cm/11x7in shallow baking tin. Put the raisins in a bowl. Warm the sherry, pour over the raisins and set aside to soak.
2 Pour the water into a bowl, sprinkle on the yeast, stir and leave to froth for 15 minutes.
3 Put the pizza mix in a large bowl, stir in 50g/2oz of the sugar and make a well in the centre. Add the frothed yeast and mix to a soft dough.
4 Turn out on to a floured surface and knead for 2-3 minutes until smooth. Drain the raisins, reserving the liquid, then knead them into the dough.
5 Press into the prepared baking tin, pushing the dough to the edges. Cover with oiled cling film and leave to rise in a warm place for about 30 minutes until doubled in height.
6 Preheat oven to 220C/fan oven 200C/Gas 7. Make dimples all over the surface of the dough with your fingers and lay the sliced figs on top. Drizzle with a little olive oil and sprinkle with the remaining sugar. Bake for 10-15 minutes until golden and caramelised.
7 Spoon the reserved sherry over the focaccia and leave to cool slightly. Serve warm, with soft goat's cheese or crème fraîche.

Topped with juicy caramelised figs, this soft sweet focaccia is made with pizza mix lightened with a little extra yeast.

Gingerbread with figs

16-20 slices

450g/1lb self-raising flour
½ tsp salt
½ tsp bicarbonate of soda
2 tsp ground ginger
115g/4oz dried figs, chopped
50g/2oz crystallised ginger, diced

225g/8oz light muscovado sugar
175g/6oz butter
175g/6oz treacle
175g/6oz golden syrup
300ml/½ pint milk
2 medium eggs, beaten

1 Preheat oven to 180C/fan oven 160C/Gas 4. Grease and line a 25cm/10in square cake tin.

2 Sift the flour, salt, bicarbonate of soda and ground ginger into a bowl. Stir in the figs and diced ginger. Make a well in the centre.

3 Put the sugar, butter, treacle, syrup and milk in a pan and heat gently until melted. Pour into the well and add the eggs. Stir to mix, then beat for 1 minute.

4 Turn the mixture into the prepared tin and bake for 1-1¼ hours until a skewer inserted in the centre comes out clean.

5 Leave in the tin for 10 minutes, then transfer to a wire rack to cool. Serve cut into fingers.

Note This cake improves with keeping. When cold, wrap in greaseproof paper, then in foil and store in a tin for 1 week.

Jamaican style gingerbread flavoured with chopped dried figs and crystallised ginger.

Cinnamon chocolate chip cookies

Illustrated on page 292

Makes 24
140g/5oz butter or margarine,
    softened
200g/7oz soft brown sugar
50g/2oz caster sugar
2 medium eggs, beaten
350g/12oz plain flour

1 tsp bicarbonate of soda
½ tsp salt
1 tsp ground cinnamon
115g/4oz chopped peanuts
2 x 115g packets plain chocolate
    drops

1 Preheat oven to 190C/fan oven 170C/Gas 5. Cream the butter and sugars together in a bowl until soft and fluffy. Beat in the eggs.
2 Sift the flour, bicarbonate of soda, salt and cinnamon together over the mixture. Beat well, then stir in the peanuts and chocolate.
3 Drop tablespoonfuls of the mixture well apart on to baking sheets lined with non-stick baking parchment and flatten slightly. Bake for 15-17 minutes until golden.
4 Leave on baking sheets for 10 minutes, then transfer cookies to a wire rack to cool.

Variation Shape smaller cookies if you prefer, reducing the cooking time by 2-3 minutes.

Giant American-style cookies – crisp on the outside, yet meltingly soft within.

Lavender and ginger cookies

Illustrated on page 293

Makes about 36

115g/4oz butter, softened

85g/3oz caster sugar

1 medium egg, beaten

1 tsp vanilla extract

1 tbsp fresh or dried lavender flowers (see note)

1 tbsp chopped preserved stem ginger

225g/8oz plain flour

¼ tsp bicarbonate of soda

½ tsp baking powder

½ tsp salt

½ tsp ground ginger

50ml/2fl oz soured cream or crème fraîche

1 Cream the butter and sugar together in a bowl until soft. Beat in the egg, vanilla and lavender, then fold in the chopped ginger.

2 Sift the flour with the bicarbonate of soda, baking powder, salt and ground ginger. Beat into the mixture, alternately with the soured cream; the dough will be quite soft.

3 Tip the dough on to a sheet of greaseproof paper and gently roll into a cylinder, about 5cm/2in thick. Wrap tightly in cling film and refrigerate for at least 6 hours, preferably overnight.

4 To bake, preheat oven to 190C/fan oven 170C/Gas 5. Slice off thin rounds from the dough as required. Place on baking sheets lined with non-stick baking parchment. Bake for 8-10 minutes until pale golden and set.

5 Cool slightly on the baking sheets, then transfer to a wire rack to cool.

Note If using dried lavender, buy a culinary grade – obtainable from herb suppliers, or dry your own flowers if you have lavender in the garden.

Exquisite fragrant cookies that can be freshly baked to order. Make the dough in advance, keep chilled, then slice and bake as required.

Carrot and raisin cookies

Illustrated on page 293

Makes about 36

225g/8oz freshly cooked carrots, drained

115g/4oz butter or margarine, softened

140g/5oz light muscovado sugar

1 large egg, beaten

400g/14oz plain flour

1½ tsp baking powder

½ tsp ground cinnamon

¼ tsp ground nutmeg

¼ tsp ground ginger

¼ tsp salt

85g/3oz seedless raisins

50g/2oz pecan nuts or walnuts, chopped

1 Preheat oven to 190C/fan oven 170C/Gas 5. Line two baking sheets with non-stick baking parchment. Dry the carrots on kitchen paper, then mash thoroughly until smooth.

2 Cream the butter and sugar together in a bowl. Add the mashed carrot and egg.

3 Sift the flour, baking powder, spices and salt over the mixture, then beat together thoroughly. Stir in the raisins and nuts.

4 Drop teaspoonfuls of the mixture on to the baking sheets, spacing well apart, then flatten the mixture with the back of a wet spoon to shape roughly into rounds. Bake for 12-15 minutes until light golden brown.

5 Leave on the baking sheet for 10 minutes, then transfer to a wire rack to cool completely.

These lightly spiced drop cookies are perfect for lunch boxes.

Vanilla thins

Makes 36

300g/10oz plain flour
1 tsp baking powder
½ tsp salt
2 vanilla pods, split
225g/8oz butter, cubed and softened
225g/8oz caster sugar
1 large egg, beaten

1 Sift the flour together with the baking powder and salt on to a sheet of greaseproof paper.
2 Scrape the seeds from the vanilla pods into the food processor. Add the butter and sugar and process until pale and fluffy. Add the egg and mix until incorporated.
3 Add the sifted flour and process briefly to a soft dough; do not overwork.
4 Turn on to a floured surface and knead lightly. Lift on to greaseproof paper and roll the dough into a cylinder, 5cm/2in thick. Wrap tightly in cling film and refrigerate for at least 6 hours, preferably overnight.
5 To bake, preheat oven to 190C/fan oven 170C/Gas 5. Slice off thin rounds from the dough as required. Place on baking sheets lined with non-stick baking parchment and bake for about 10 minutes until golden and set. Cool slightly on the baking sheets, then transfer to a wire rack to cool.

Note This cookie dough will keep tightly wrapped in the fridge for up to 1 week.

Flavoured with real vanilla seeds, these delicate biscuits make an elegant treat to serve with coffee or ice cream.

Coconut and blueberry cakes

Makes 8
115g/4oz unsalted butter, at room
   temperature
115g/4oz caster sugar
2 tbsp milk

2 large eggs, lightly beaten
85g/3oz self-raising flour
½ tsp baking powder
85g/3oz desiccated coconut
140g/5oz blueberries

1 Preheat oven to 180C/fan oven 160C/Gas 4. Line a muffin tray with 8 paper muffin cases.
2 Cream the butter and sugar together in a bowl until pale and fluffy, then stir in the milk. Beat in the eggs, a little at a time.
3 Sift the flour and baking powder together over the mixture, add the coconut and fold in carefully. Gently fold in most of the blueberries and spoon into the paper cases.
4 Scatter the remaining blueberries on top and bake for 20-25 minutes until firm to the touch. Cool on a wire rack.

Deliciously moist, fruity buns dotted with fresh blueberries.

Index

Acknowledgements

The publishers wish to thank the following for the loan of props for photography:
The Conran Shop, Michelin House, 81 Fulham Road, London SW3 (0207 589 7401); **Divertimenti**, 139-141 Fulham Road, London SW3 (0207 581 8065); **Divertimenti**, 45-7 Wigmore Street, London W1 (0207 935 0689); **Designers Guild**, 277 Kings Road, London SW3 (0207 351 5775); **Habitat**, 196 Tottenham Court Road, London W1 (0207 631 3880); **Ikea**, Purley Way, Croydon (0208 208 5607); **Inventory**, 26-40 Kensington High Street, London W8 (0207 937 2626); **Jerry's**, 163-7 Fulham Road, London SW3 (0207 581 0909); **LSA International**, The Dolphin Estate, Windmill Road, Sunbury on Thames, Middlesex (01932 789 721); **Muji**, 26 Great Marlborough Street, London W1 (0207 494 1197)

Food Stylists Maxine Clark, Joanna Farrow, Marie Ange Lapierre, Louise Pickford, Bridget Sargeson, Linda Tubby
Photographic Stylists Kasha Harmer Hirst, Maya Babic
Contributors Sara Buenfeld, Maxine Clark, Joanna Farrow, Janet Illsley, Louise Pickford, Bridget Sargeson, Linda Tubby, Sunil Vijayakar